THE HOLINESS OF PASCAL.

Mon pere s'est servi de ce corps de droit pour son ouvrage des trois cercles

portrai de Mr pascal fait par mon pere

THE HOLINESS OF PASCAL.

BY

H. F. STEWART, B.D.

FELLOW AND DEAN OF ST JOHN'S COLLEGE, CAMBRIDGE.

THE HULSEAN LECTURES 1914–15.

Cambridge:
at the University Press,
1915.

CAMBRIDGE UNIVERSITY PRESS
Cambridge, New York, Melbourne, Madrid, Cape Town,
Singapore, São Paulo, Delhi, Mexico City

Cambridge University Press
The Edinburgh Building, Cambridge CB2 8RU, UK

Published in the United States of America by Cambridge University Press, New York

www.cambridge.org
Information on this title: www.cambridge.org/9781107628946

First published 1915
First paperback edition 2013

A catalogue record for this publication is available from the British Library

ISBN 978-1-107-62894-6 Paperback

IN · MEMORIAM

VIRI · DESIDERATISSIMI

IOHANNIS · E · B · MAYOR

MISERICORDIAE · ET · VERITATIS · AMICI

QVI · IPSE · QVANTVM · NEMO · ALIVS

CONCIONES · VERO · CHRISTI · SPIRITV · INSTINCTAS

NOTIS · ERVDITISSIMIS · ILLVSTRARE · SCIEBAT

HOC · OPUS · QVANTVLVMCVMQVE

DEDICAVIT

AUCTOR

PREFACE.

HULSEAN LECTURES are partly lectures and partly sermons, and are liable to the defects of either kind. They certainly do not gain from being read in cold blood. But despite their ambiguous character and Pascal's frequent warnings against mixing the Orders, these Lecture-Sermons for 1914–1915 are here printed just as they were delivered, save for some slight verbal changes and the restoration of a few passages which my watch warned me to drop.

Seven days elapsed between the first and second lectures, seven days between the third and fourth, and seven weeks between the second and third. This will partly account for the incoherence and the repetitions, of which I am fully conscious. The few topical allusions may help the future librarian to date the volume if the moth spares more than the title-page. The book has no pretension to do more than clear away some current misconceptions about the work and character of a great Christian and a great genius and suggest some thoughts regarding his present value.

The first of these objects has been rendered easy by the completion of the collected works in the series of *Les Grands Écrivains de la France* and especially by the recent publication of two books (1) F. Strowski's *Pascal et son temps,* 3 vols. (Paris 1908), and (2) E. Jovy's *Pascal Inédit,* 5 vols. (Vitry-le-François 1908–1912). Reflexions of M. Strowski's book are visible on most of my pages; M. Jovy's researches may be said to have revolutionized the study of Pascal.

In estimating Pascal's present influence I have been much helped by Père L. Laberthonnière's "L'Apologétique de Pascal" in his *Essais de Philosophie religieuse* (Paris, *s.d.* but 1903).

The principal editions of the *Pensées* are mentioned below in the text; the *Lettres Provinciales* may be studied in the learned edition of J. De Soyres (1880).

Among works indispensable to the *Pascalisant* are A. Vinet's *Études sur Pascal* (1848); Sully Prudhomme's *La vraie Religion selon Pascal* (1905); É. Boutroux's *Pascal* (1907); J. Paquier's *Le Jansénisme* (1909). None of these however renders otiose the perusal of Sainte-Beuve's immortal *Port-Royal,* of which volumes III and IV are chiefly devoted to Pascal and his family.

Of English studies on Pascal there is good store, e.g. Henry Rogers's *Edinburgh Review* article (1847), Dean Church's illuminating Sermon (1875), Principal Tulloch's *Pascal* (Foreign Classics for English readers (1878)),

Viscount St Cyres' *Pascal* (1909), H. T. Morgan's *Port Royal and other studies* (1914), pp. 111–129[1].

In deference to a wish expressed by several of my hearers I have added a number of notes in a place where the reader can escape them if he will. Some are meant to serve as *pièces justificatives* for disputable assertions in the text, others to shew what Pascal really said.

The interesting portrait which I am able to reproduce, by kind permission of Messrs Hachette and Co., is by Pascal's friend, the distinguished lawyer, Jean Domat (1625–96). The original is in red chalk, and was drawn, as his son tells us, on a blank page of a *Corpus Juris Civilis*[2].

I am greatly indebted to the Master of Peterhouse and Mr Arthur Tilley for general help and advice, to Signor R. Piccoli for references to Campanella, and to the printers and readers of the University Press for the speed and care with which they have executed what I fear was a troublesome piece of work in what I know are difficult times.

[1] The late Dr Paget, Bishop of Oxford, projected a volume of thoughts on the *Thoughts*, and prepared a notebook for the purpose. *Pendent opera interrupta.* (See *Life*, 1912, p. 312.)

[2] Domat's *Les lois civiles dans leur ordre naturel* was first published in 1694.

H. F. S.

May 1915.

CONTENTS.

I

Mercy and Truth are met together: Righteousness and Peace have kissed each other. Psalm lxxxv. 10.

THIS psalm is a prayer for the restoration of Israel and a prophecy of blessings to come. Jehovah has been merciful and has brought His people out of captivity. He has put away His wrath and forgiven them all their sin. Such news is too good to be true, and hope falls back into deprecation. God's anger is still drawn out. Will He not raise up His chosen again and give them cause to praise Him? The answer comes quick upon the cry. The Lord speaks comfort and promises salvation—outward wealth, springing from the marriage of Mercy and Truth, issuing in Righteousness and Peace. God will make His way plain, a holy way for men to walk in.

The picture is primarily a social one—the psalm is a national psalm; but it has a personal application. The Mercy and the Truth which are promised to the people are the prerogative of God Himself, and He imparts them to individuals as well as to nations. They are indeed the very qualities by which He revealed Himself to Moses when He made all His goodness pass before him. Not as omnipotent, omniscient, omnipresent was He proclaimed, but as a God full of compassion and gracious, slow to anger, plenteous in Mercy and Truth.

The sum of God's character is Mercy and Truth, and

it must be that His saints should shew some reflexion of the beauty of Him who has called them and set them apart. If a man have not this, he is not really a saint; if he have it ever so faintly, then we see that he is at least marked for service.

I propose in these lectures to deal, however perfunctorily, with one who bore this sacred sign, who deserves, if ever man did, to be called saint, Blaise Pascal. He was far from perfect; he was headstrong and impatient, he long clung to the things which he came to think were hateful; but his mind was aflame for Truth, and his heart athirst for Christ and His poor. And the Mercy which he practised and the Truth which he loved brought, in the end, to his frail body and his restless intellect, a Peace which the world could not give and a Righteousness which he would have been the last to claim for himself. The mercy may be gathered from his sister's account of his last days: examples of it will come up as we talk about him, examples which by their mixture of charity and common sense effectually dispel the legend that he was a misanthrope or a maniac[1]. But the best measure of his mercy, and not only of his mercy but of his truth, his weakness, and his strength, is contained in one of his own *Pensées*, in words so sacred that unless they can be proved false, they assuredly proclaim him saint.

"I love all men as my brethren because they are redeemed. I love poverty because He loved it. I love money because it gives the means of helping the miserable. I keep troth with all. I do not render evil to those who wrong me, but I wish them a lot like mine which brings neither good nor harm from men. I try to be just (he first wrote I keep faithfulness and justice), true, sincere and faithful towards all men; and I have a tender heart for those whom God has more closely bound to me; and whether I am alone or seen of men, I lay all my actions before God, who shall judge them, and to whom I have consecrated them. These are my thoughts, and every day of my life I bless God my Redeemer who has implanted them in me and who has transformed a man full of weakness, misery, concupiscence, pride, and ambition into one exempt from all these evils through the power of His Grace, to which all the glory is due, since of myself I have but misery and error[2]."

If this is not the heart of a saint speaking out of its fulness, it is the heart of a hypocrite. My business will be to prove that it is a saint's.

I do not propose to tell Pascal's story in detail, but there are three points in it which are so liable to be missed that we must deal with them in order to understand the man. Of these points two are of a negative, and one of a positive, character. First, Pascal was not of the inner circle of Port-Royal—he was never a Solitary. Secondly, he did not, when he turned to religion, turn his back for ever on mathematics. Lastly, he was a man of wealth and position. It is this last fact which, coupled with his extraordinary scientific attainment, gives peculiar interest to his Christianity. If, as we are sometimes assured, saints are rare among men of science, they are rarer still among men of the world. So it is of this last point that I shall treat first.

Blaise Pascal came of a good Auvergnat stock, ennobled in the course of the fifteenth century, and furnishing several generations of useful civil servants[3]. His father held an important fiscal position at Clermont[4]. When the boy was eight years old, Étienne Pascal, already a widower[5], retired from his post in Auvergne and came to Paris. His money was well invested, and he could devote himself without anxiety to the pursuit of science and the education of his three children[6]. Everyone knows the story of the marvellous boyhood of Blaise, and how he proved the first thirty-two propositions of Euclid by the light of nature. The tale may have gained rather than lost on the lips of his admiring elder sister[7], but it is quite characteristic of the man who took nothing at second hand, that the child should have embarked on a voyage of mathematical discovery.

The circle of his father's acquaintance in Paris included men of note in the social as well as in the scientific world, and the success of his little sister Jacqueline as a prodigy of infant versification brought the family before the notice of the Queen, and of a greater than either Queen or King. It was indeed through her innocent intervention at an afternoon party[8] that her father passed from under the displeasure of the great Cardinal who then ruled France[9], into his high favour and a fresh place of trust. Richelieu forgave him and sent him into Normandy as *Intendant* or royal commissioner of finance. The move to Rouen was crucial for the Pascals in more ways than one. It was here that they first saw that form of religion with which their name is indissolubly connected. Jansenist doctrine and practice were being sedulously furthered in Normandy by the good *curé* of Rouville[10]. He drew crowds to his sermons and made many converts. Among them were two excellent gentlemen, philanthropists and amateur bone-setters, who were called in by M. Pascal when he broke his thigh one slippery January day in 1646. They cured his leg and they opened his mind to the beauties of Jansen, Saint-Cyran, Arnauld and others of the clan. Étienne was touched, but not so deeply as his son. Blaise converted Jacqueline, and they two between them finished the work which the healers had begun upon their father[11]; the married sister and her husband from Clermont followed their example, and by the end of the year all five were more or less under Jansenist direction. That the fervour or consistency of the women of the family was greater than the men's, will appear in the sequel; but on any shewing the atmosphere which Blaise breathed all these years was one of high thinking. The living, on the other hand, was not particularly plain. Rouen was at that time in point of culture hardly inferior to Paris[12], and the King's *Intendant* was naturally a leader in society. Rouen was a school of the fashionable philosophy of the day, a Christianized stoicism[13]; it was a very nursery of men of letters; it was the home of Pierre Corneille, who knew the Pascals well, who set the pattern for Jacqueline's verses and congratulated her in public when she won an annual prize for poetry[14].

This was in fact just the society where the lad of twenty would acquire the tastes which his Jansenist friends and he himself lamented later, and would nurse ambitions which, if harmless, were strictly speaking worldly. He devised a calculating machine, intended primarily no doubt to help his father in his office-work, but probably also to bring profit to the inventor, for he meant to put it on the market, and he protected it by a royal privilege[15]. This instrument, which it took him years to perfect, of which he explained the mechanism in the drawing-room of a great lady and dedicated the completed model to a crowned head, involved expenses of production only possible to a long purse. Still further evidence of money easy to command and readily spent on science, is supplied by the experiments which he undertook in order to prove the pressure of the atmosphere. Research of this kind was very costly in the seventeenth century, and whereas rival experimenters in the same field had to be content with four feet of glass tubes or wooden pipes, Pascal is able in a lordly way to commission two glass tubes each forty feet long, and wine in proportion, wherewith to convince his gainsayers[16]. In a word he early learnt the value of money and loved it for what it brought—not at this time as the means of relieving misery, but as the means of advancing knowledge and winning fame and fortune.

He had his reward. At fifteen he was already famous, being recommended to Richelieu as a boy "very learned in mathematics[17]"; at sixteen he composed a treatise on Conic Sections which was received with astonishment and incredulity by Descartes; and now at the age of twenty-three he had made a sensible advance towards the solution of a capital problem in physical science. What might he not expect if health—a doubtful factor, for he was very delicate—and wealth were preserved to him! No wonder that when his generous father died and his property was divided up, Blaise regretted to see his younger sister's portion on the point of disappearing into the common chest of the Port-Royal convent. Her decision to take the veil was indeed not new to him; he had himself shewn her the way; he had sympathized with her in the little difficulties she had had with their father when the project was first broached. But the moment she now chose for its fulfilment was very inconvenient, with so much precious work on hand and a position to make and maintain. If she joined forces with him they would do well; if she withdrew he would be seriously straitened. It is probable that the succession was saddled with certain family obligations[18] In a couple of years the situation would be easier, the arithmetical machine might be in general use and provide an income. So he urged her at least to wait this space. Madame Perier, the married sister, backed him up. His suggestion was reasonable and legally correct; it did no material harm to Jacqueline, but it hurt her feelings sorely. She was disappointed in her brother. Not so her friends at Port-Royal. The convent was then ruled by the Abbess Angélique Arnauld, with her sister Agnès at her right hand and M. Singlin for her confessor. They all knew Blaise—Singlin at least in person, the nuns by reputation—and they had their own opinion about his devotion to science and other mundane vanities. *La Mère Angélique* in particular (who dominates the whole of this little drama, a figure of extraordinary beauty and sagacity), as she comforted the weeping girl, holding her to her bosom for a whole hour, spoke of him very plainly as belonging to the world and too frivolous to prefer an act of charity before his personal convenience. Nothing short of a miracle could touch him, "I mean a miracle of nature and affection, for there is no reason to look for a miracle of Grace in a person like him, and you know one must never count on miracles[19]." But if the Mother Superior is great on this occasion, Pascal is not contemptible, and the end of it was that as soon as he saw his sister's distress with his own eyes, he gave way, and the last scene is one of conflicting renunciations—Jacqueline, at the prompting of her abbess, eager to forgo her share, Blaise, moved by brotherly affection—the mother was right, Grace was not yet at work—pressing her to take it up. And here again the admirable nun displays her wisdom and her charity. "If Blaise is acting from Christian motives, the convent will accept—but not otherwise; we have learnt from M. de Saint-Cyran to take nothing for God's House but that which comes from God." Blaise signed the contract then and there, and after this glimpse into a world of which for all his Rouen and Rouville experiences he was not yet worthy, went back into the other world, to his arithmetical machine and his wealthy friends.

The society in which he moved was what the century called *celle des honnêtes gens,* people of refinement and breeding, whose code was that of *les bienséances* or good manners—perhaps the highest merely social code that has ever existed. It was the code by which Mme de Rambouillet softened and sweetened the rough manners of the early century[20]. No one who rebelled against it was admitted to her salon, and it was no mere collection of external rules. The cynical La Rochefoucauld allowed its sanction and has analysed it for us. "It is the duty of an *honnête homme* to find pleasure in the pleasure of others, to treat their self-love with consideration and to avoid wounding it." "The intercourse of *honnêtes gens* cannot subsist without some measure of mutual confidence." "You must anticipate the pleasures of others, seek out ways of serving them, share their heartaches and, when these cannot be averted, shew them sympathy." These maxims were penned some ten years after the time with which we are engaged[21], but the man who largely inspired La Rochefoucauld and who was the acknowledged arbiter of *honnêteté* was the Chevalier de Méré, scholar, freethinker, wit, purist, and gambler. Here is his confession of Faith. "I love Paris, the court, the gaming-table, music, ballets, the conversation of a gentleman and of a pretty woman; but losing these I do not count all lost; other pleasures come to console me. I love the song of birds in the copse, the prattle of a clear stream, the voices of the flocks in the fields. All this conveys to me a quiet and natural peace[22]." This man was one of Pascal's intimate associates. Another was Damien Mitton, a somewhat shadowy figure, who nevertheless stands in Paseal's mind and in his *Pensées* as the type of the worldling, disillusioned, pessimistic, who answers every endeavour with a shrug and an "Is it worth while?", whose motto is deportment and his object the avoidance of unnecessary trouble. Another, of higher birth and better purpose, was the young Duc de Roannez, hereditary governor of Poitou, a great amateur of mathematics, who attached Pascal to his train, or rather attached himself to Pascal and stood by him through life, who was converted to Jansenism after him, to the great disgust of his people, and helped to bring out the first edition of the *Pensées*[23].

The intricacies of the arithmetical machine were expounded, as I have said, to a great lady, the Duchesse d'Aiguillon[24], and an aristocratic crowd, and the perfected model was offered to Christina of Sweden; but of the famous women to whom Pascal paid homage—it may be said at once that no breath of scandal ever touched him—the best known was the Marquise de Sablé, who had been beautiful in her youth and was brilliant all her life, La Rochefoucauld's loyal friend, the real successor of Madame de Rambouillet, whose outward adherence to Jansenism and spasmodic retreats at Port-Royal never changed her worldly heart and were the despair of the Abbess[25].

There is no question that for a time Pascal's life was that of an *honnête homme* among *honnêtes gens*, that it was marked by a splendour answering to his fame, that he played a part in Vanity Fair, that he knew at first-hand some of the distractions whose emptiness he condemns in the *Pensées*—the gaming-table, the chase, the tennis-court, feminine conversation—and from his friends the fascination of war and office of state[26]. And his zest must have been the keener for the shortness of the time, eighteen months, during which he followed them[27]. It was his way to do nothing by halves. The recoil came suddenly, though the conversion to which it led was not yet. Towards the end of 1653 he was seized by a great contempt for the world and with an ill-contained disgust with those who are of it. That it was not a true conversion appears from the account of his visit to his sister (now La Sœur Jacqueline de Sainte-Euphémie) at Port-Royal nine or ten months later, in September 1654.

This must be given in her own words. "He came to see me, and on this visit he opened his heart to me in a way that moved me greatly, confessing that amid his important occupations and all the things which helped to make him love the world and which were with reason supposed to have great hold on him, he was urgently prompted to quit it all both by the extreme distaste he had for unholy follies and distractions, and by the constant pricking of his conscience; that he felt detached from things in a way he had never been before, nor anything like it; but that yet he was so completely deserted by God that he felt no drawing in that direction: that nevertheless he was reaching out thither with all his might, feeling all the time that it was much more his intellect and his human spirit that were impelling him towards what he knew to be best than the Spirit of God, and that if he only had in his present state of detachment the feelings towards God which once he had, he thought he could undertake anything, and that he must have then been terribly bound to the world to be able to resist the gracious impulses and movements which God was bestowing on him[28]." Terribly bound to the world! What were the bonds that were holding him? Not, we may be sure, only the shows and gauds of society, although we know that he kept his carriage and horses, his staff of servants, his fine furniture, his books and his plate, until within two years of his death[29]. But Pascal, though an *honnête homme*, was also and above all a man of science, and it is rather in science than in pleasure that he buried those former feelings about God. Like many men before and since, he strove, it would seem, to deaden doubt by work. At any rate the two years 1653–1654 are the period of his most fruitful mathematical discoveries. These are contained in his treatises on the *Arithmetical Triangle*, on *Numerical Orders* and eight others, presented to "the Illustrious Paris Academy of Mathematics" (whatever that exactly was)[30]. He used the Arithmetical Triangle to solve the "Problem of Points" in behalf of his gamester friend Méré, and his correspondence with Fermat, arising out of this question, marks an epoch in the history of the Theory of Probability[31].

It is to this same period that may most probably be assigned, if it be genuine, a *Discourse on the Passions of*

Love, a project of marrying and settling down, if ever it was really formed[32]; and with much greater certainty, a deeper study of the philosophers Epictetus and Montaigne his first acquaintance with whom no doubt went back to the Rouen days.

But neither science nor philosophy could bring him peace. The cry of his soul was that of St Augustine's: *irrequietum est cor nostrum donec requiescat in te.* He was very ill; he saw in the return and increase of his infirmities the visible hand of God. He wrote a long and passionate prayer[33], asking forgiveness for his failures, and grace to bear his punishment with patience. He had his answer. In a mystic vision of two midnight hours on November 23, 1654, there was revealed to him in a light of fire[34] the living God, purging his sins by His pity, filling him with certitude, love, and joy, coming to dwell with him and rendering him incapable of any end but Himself. The Lord laid His hand upon him, he saw unspeakable things. Such a call brooked no delay. Quick, the world must be quitted and all its perilous attachments. He shook them off with a rapidity that astonished his sister, who thought he must still for some time bear upon him traces of the mire in which he had floundered[35]. A few visits to Paris to set his affairs in order, and he is ready for his retreat. We shall speak of his outward and inward history at Port-Royal presently. For the moment it is enough to say that he put himself without reserve into the hands of his directors, M. Singlin and M. de Saci, and that by the *Provincial Letters* he repaid them magnificently for what they did for him. These Letters could assuredly not have been written but by a man who knew the world.

They prove the value of his training and experience there And when they were done, or as much of them as he chose to do, and while in the intervals of heavy sickness he was collecting materials for his *magnum opus*, the Apology for Christianity, Pascal was still the *honnête homme*, and once again the mathematician. Such glimpses as we get from the learned correspondence of the day shew that, though he had ostensibly forsworn geometry and regarded mathematics as useless[36], he was still ready to answer questions and solve problems, especially those connected with Probability[37]; and presently we find that an unforeseen occasion (his sister Mme Perier says it was a bout of toothache) led him to attack what was then considered one of the most difficult of problems, that of the cycloid and its properties, and to engage in heated controversy over it—controversy which so exhausted him that he had to rest for the better part of a year. What returned to him together with some measure of health was not his old delight in mathematics, but a desire for cultured society. Fermat, the famous geometer who had helped him with the problem of Points, was not only a very great mathematician, but a sound lawyer, a Grecian, and between whiles a poet. When Fermat writes from Toulouse suggesting that they might meet, Pascal replies that he cannot think of letting Fermat come to him, and that as he is himself not fit to move, the meeting must be postponed. This he regrets deeply, not because Fermat is the greatest mathematician in Europe, but because he is *le plus galant homme du monde*[38]. It is the wit and charm of his conversation that attracts Pascal and not his geometry. The letter contains hints of the grave occupations which have taken the place of science in

Pascal's affections. But it is noteworthy that these occupations have not killed the fine gentleman in him, and that he is not ashamed to let this be known.

We heard just now La Rochefoucauld's description of *honnêteté*. By a fortunate chance there has been preserved to us a summary of three Addresses which Pascal made for a boy of high family[39] on the duties of his position and which reduce *honnêteté* to its ultimate principles. The young noble must be under no illusion. Rank is not everything; it is not the highest order; that is the order of charity, which Pascal leaves to other teachers. But rank is something; it is an order, it deserves consideration. Pascal shews what kind of consideration, and points the way in which a man of exalted rank must qualify for the worthier consideration that waits on *honnêteté*. He admits that it is not a way that carries a man very far. "If you do not get beyond it, you will infallibly lose your soul, but at least you will lose it like a gentleman[40]." A duke is not necessarily an *honnête homme*; but as duke he will always merit and get outward respect. He must see to it that he wins esteem as *honnête homme*.

Pascal's method is strictly mathematical; he deals with one thing at a time, he refuses to mix his orders. What the boy needs is instruction in that very valuable matter of *honnêteté*, and never was the theme of "noblesse oblige" developed more convincingly.

To the end, or very nearly to the end, of his life, Pascal remained in touch with his great friends and kept a window open upon the world. He recovered the taste for wealth and the art of making it, but this time not for himself; he had abjured all personal luxury and sold even all his books except his Bible, his St Augustine and perhaps Montaigne[41]. So when his practical genius revealed to him the possibilities of the public vehicle which he called *carrosse à cinq sous* and we call the omnibus, he devoted all his profits in the company to the famine-stricken poor of Blois and to the Paris Infirmary[42].

Instances might be multiplied; but I have, I think, said enough to establish two of my points, viz. that Pascal never let go his hold on mathematics and, that saint and ascetic as he was, he was also a man of the world.

The other point is rather more delicate and touches nearly the question of Pascal's Truth. His name is so inseparably tied to Port-Royal, his defence of Port-Royal and all it stood for is so complete and wholehearted, that it is difficult to take him at his word when in the *Provincial Letters* he declares that their writer is not of Port-Royal[43]. In order to clear him we must see what Port-Royal was and what the qualification, "of Port-Royal," involves.

Port-Royal was a Cistercian convent, twenty odd miles from Paris, with a branch house in the city. It had been roused from lethargy early in the century by its child superior Jacqueline Arnauld (in religion *la Mère Angélique*)[44], and inspired or infected with Jansenism by its director the Abbé de Saint-Cyran, Jansen's friend and lieutenant in their joint attempt to recover for Christianity primitive purity of doctrine and life. Jansen dealt especially with doctrine, Saint-Cyran especially with conduct.

The nuns, dear saints, did not trouble themselves greatly with questions of theology. They took their opinions from their director. The theological weight of

Port-Royal lay in the ecclesiastics and laymen who were known as the Solitaries of Port-Royal. The Solitaries were in no sense a religious Order; they were bound by no vows except those which their conscience dictated; they were simply men who had renounced the world for a life of retreat, of prayer and penitence, of meditation and study. They lived in proximity to the Convent, first in Paris and later at Port-Royal des Champs. Some of them worked with their hands, others conducted a school for boys, *les Petites Écoles*, of which Tillemont and Racine are the most famous pupils and which count for much in the history of pedagogy[45]. The Solitaries were all ardent disciples of Saint-Cyran, and therefore followers of Jansen and pledged to the Augustinian theory of Grace as proclaimed by him. These are the men, "ces messieurs," who were generally said and understood to be "of Port-Royal." Their distinctive note was complete renunciation of the world. Now we have spent a good deal of time in shewing that Pascal never completely severed himself from the world, and the fact is that the Solitaries never looked upon him as one of themselves. Fontaine, their contemporary and faithful historian, in his account of Pascal and Port-Royal at the time of the miracle of the Holy Thorn, expressly distinguishes him from the Solitaries[46]. No doubt Pascal, when after his conversion he went into retreat with them, endeavoured to practise their virtues, sharing their studies, interesting himself in their school. But even at this period he was as much in Paris as he was at Port-Royal des Champs, living in his own house, or at a inn as M. de Mons. Although he was penetrated with their doctrine and devoted to their cause, he could with perfect truth deny that he was one of them any more than, say, his friend the Duc de Luynes[47], who was a notable supporter of Port-Royal without being in the technical and recognized sense "of it."

And Pascal came to part company with them. I do not believe that the breach was so profound and entire as the opponents of Jansenism began to assert within a few years of Pascal's death, or as has been maintained recently with exceptional ability and vigour[48]. I do not believe that he ever abjured Jansenism or the Jansenists. But that there was a definite rift, a conflict of opinion between them, is plain and is admitted; and that there was a subsequent modification of his principles is probable and is indeed supported by very good evidence. The occasion of the rift was the notorious "Formulary," imagined in 1657 and finally fixed in 1661 by the Assembly of Clergy, which required all ecclesiastical persons to "condemn with heart and lips the Five Propositions of Cornelius Jansen contained in that part of his *Augustinus* which the two Popes Innocent X and Alexander VII have condemned—which doctrine is not that of St Augustine, wrongly expounded by Jansen contrary to the true sense of that holy doctor[49]."

The heresy involved in the Five Propositions is briefly, that Grace does not belong to all men and that Christ did not die for all men. The Jesuits asserted that the Propositions were truly drawn out of the *Augustinus*; the Jansenists asserted that the Jesuits had invented them, and they defied the accusers to produce chapter and verse for their charge. We shall deal with the book and its contents later. For our present purpose it is enough to say that this document, the Formulary, was more definite and precise than anything that had preceded it. It dotted the i's of the Papal utterances which it enforced. It stated that Jansen in claiming Augustine's doctrine had deliberately distorted it. The dilemma confronting the nuns and their advisers was a thorny one. It was a choice between schism and heresy. Refusal to sign meant excommunication. Consent to sign meant the surrender of Jansen, of Saint-Cyran, and of their doctrine of Grace, which was Augustine's. The *Messieurs* of Port-Royal had to find a way out for the nuns and themselves, and, not without the connivance of Retz, Archbishop of Paris, who was sympathetic[50], they concocted a preamble to the Formulary, which declared that while signature implied hearty submission on the doctrinal points, it did not commit the signatories to more than a respectful silence on the question of fact, viz. whether or no the Propositions were really contained in the *Augustinus.* It was ingenious, but it was not sincere, and one nun at least had the courage to declare what many of her fellows had the wit to see. Pascal's sister, Sainte-Euphémie, would have none of it. "It is only the truth that maketh free" she cried, "and it only frees those who themselves set it free by openly confessing it." This device is unworthy of those who are ready to defend the truth with their lives—it recalls the Jesuits "who allow incense to be offered to an idol because of a cross you have up your sleeve[51]." Her protest has the force and irony of the *Lettres Provinciales.* But she had not the strength to carry out her convictions, and she signed. She died of it, but she signed. Her passion for Truth if not her spirit of obedience moved her brother too. When, the projected preamble being quashed by the Pope, the *Messieurs* of Port-Royal thought the nuns could sign if they added a postscript *quoad dogmata,*

Pascal roundly declared that no compromise, whether at the head or the tail of the Formulary, would serve. Doctrine and fact were here inseparable. To condemn Jansen would be to condemn St Augustine and St Paul. The Formulary must not be signed by those who cared for Truth. The middle way proposed was abominable before God, contemptible in the eyes of men, and sovranly useless[52].

Nicole and Arnauld took up the challenge, not unkindly (Arnauld indeed exhibits an elephantine playfulness)[53], but not without reference to the XVIIth *Provincial Letter* where, as we shall have occasion to note next time, Pascal had allowed the very principle of distinguishing between fact and doctrine, which he now rejected. And they pressed him by word of mouth. The Solitaries met in force at his lodgings to thresh the question out; Arnauld and Nicole had their way. Pascal exhausted himself (it was one of his bad days), trying to make them feel what he felt. Despite his weakness he had expressed himself with great vehemence, and he suddenly fainted. The company melted away, leaving him with two or three of his family. When he came to himself, his sister asked him how it had happened. He answered, "When I saw these men giving way, whom I regarded as those to whom God had revealed the truth and who ought to be its champions, I confess that I was so distressed that I could not hold out[54]." But he was not the man to accept defeat, and presently the Port-Royalists found the hand that had penned the *Little Letters* in their defence turned against themselves. Of the series of letters which he wrote, accusing them of shiftiness in dealing with Grace, we know little more than what Nicole tells us, writing five years after their appearance[55]. If we may believe his critic, Pascal did not properly verify the reference supplied to him, was shaky in his dates, and blind to the Jansenists' really consistent attitude towards Grace. We need to check Nicole's charges by the letters themselves, and this alas! is impossible. They were only meant for publication in case the nuns signed the Formulary. If they refused, the letters were to be burnt. And no doubt burnt they were, for by this time the order had gone forth requiring instant signature without any sort of qualification or reserve[56]. And that neither Nicole nor Arnauld nor any friend of Port-Royal could recommend.

We may well believe that Pascal had lost his grip. But we must remember that he was dying, physically incapable of prolonged mental effort, and preparing almost feverishly for his departure, *ἐρῶν τοῦ ἀποθανεῖν.* But if death was filming the eye that had looked so steadily on the Truth, it could not quench the Mercy in his heart. We turn with relief from these acrid passages to Pascal's touching efforts literally to embrace poverty—begging for a poor companion to be cared for and treated like himself, or at least that they would send him to die in the Hospital among the poor[57]; and we read with an emotion that the lost Letters against the Jansenists could not evoke his last words to the priest who heard his last confession and administered his last Communion. He groaned to see divisions among the faithful which prejudiced the cause of charity and unity, and to see arms that should be used against real infidels and heretics serving in fratricidal conflict. With regard to the difficult questions of Grace and Predestination, on which the battle turned, he was content to cry, *O altitudo!*[58]

One of his latest recorded acts of mercy points towards a softening of his Jansenist prejudices. As he was coming from hearing Mass at St-Sulpice one morning, he was accosted by a poor girl asking alms. He enquired into her case and took her there and then to the seminary attached to the church, where he entrusted her to the care of a good priest and provided clothes and funds to place her in a suitable situation. The incident acquires extraordinary significance when we realize that St-Sulpice was, if not a Jesuit, at least an anti-Jansenist church, and that the seminary had been founded by M. Olier, who detested Jansenism and called it a monster[59]. It is clear that Pascal was not known to the priest who received him and his foundling—nor to any of the house; but it is also clear that he was not afraid of deserting his own parish church and going to mass in a church which a thorough Port-Royalist would have avoided like a Lazaret. This certainly does not compel us to write down his sister, Madame Perier, a liar, when she says that he never broke with his Port-Royal friends, that they came to visit him when he lay dying, and that he made his confession to one of them[60]. But it shews what his talk with his other confessor has already indicated, that he was rising above party spirit, and that if to the last he remembered and spoke of the *Provincial Letters* without regret[61], it was not because they had served a party aim, but because in them he had struck a blow for what he believed then and still believed to be the essential truth.

Next Sunday we shall see Pascal in controversy. But to-day as we stand by his death-bed and watch the tears of gratitude flow for the crowning mercy of his last sacrament, the gift so greatly desired of the Body broken for him; as we hear the last words he uttered before his senses left him, "May God never abandon me"—the great truths for which he fought turn to littleness and are lost in the glory of the presence of a true and faithful Creator; the mercy he was allowed to practise pales before the loving-kindness of the most merciful Saviour whose Hands were ready to receive his soul made precious, we believe, in His sight, purged from the defilement of the world, and presented pure to Him through the marvellous working of His Grace, whose judgments Pascal with St Paul confessed to be "unsearchable and His ways past finding out.

II

My text is still Mercy and Truth; my theme is Pascal in Controversy.

There is a wonderful page in Madame de Sévigné's letters, describing a passage of arms between the poet Boileau and a Jesuit father, some thirty years after Pascal's death. Talk is running on the topic of the ancients and moderns. Boileau, partisan of the ancients, is pressed to give the name of the one modern whom he has just declared to be better than all, ancients or moderns alike. He refuses, until, harassed by his questioner, he takes him by the arm, squeezes it, and says "If you *will* know, it's Pascal." The Jesuit, flushing red with surprise, blurts out a disparaging epithet. At this the poet boils over. He rushes up and down like a madman, and finally bolts into the dining-room, refusing to look at the man who dared to call Pascal "false[62]". If the Jesuit had said that Pascal was wrong, it is possible that Boileau would have shewn equal vehemence, but perhaps he would have condescended to argument: Pascal's story provides matter for debate even after two hundred and fifty years. But to-day we may repel more calmly but with no less confidence the charge of moral or intellectual dishonesty, and it is our business to do so this afternoon.

There was full opportunity for the charge during Pascal's lifetime. He was always in controversy of one sort or another, scientific or theological—not always for his own hand; his hardest blows were dealt in defence of his friends. But his proud and impatient nature, his nerves which constant illness had strung to cracking-point, a fierce zeal for truth and an astonishing gift of dialectic—all this led him to engage frequently; and, once engaged, there is no doubt that he enjoyed it.

His first great quarrel, like his last but one, was with a Jesuit, and that in a sphere where theology played no part. Father Noël, rector of a Jesuit college[63], with a taste for science and a scholastic training, endeavoured bravely to reconcile the ancient system of physics with the new. He was a friend of Descartes, but he held firmly to the time-old doctrine that Nature abhors a vacuum. Pascal, who was acquainted with recent Italian experiments on the pressure of the atmosphere, though he did not know by whom they were made[64], had himself experimented extensively on his own account, and had come to the conclusion that, although a vacuum was abhorrent to Nature, it was not impossible. He published his results in 1647 and at once got into touch with Noël. There was a smart debate between them, marked by perfect courtesy, until an unfortunate book by Noël came out, which he was too sick to revise and which seemed to reassert all the points he had already ceded[65]. Pascal's father blundered in with a letter which shewed his dislike of the Jesuits even more clearly than his love for science, and Pascal himself was moved to speak a few plain words[66]. Father Noël was an amiable old gentleman who bore no grudge. He was indeed lavish with praise for the youth who had worsted him[67]. But it is obvious that Pascal's first contact with the Society of Jesus was not of a kind to give him a high opinion of their consistency or of their science. Nor is it surprising that when, four years later, he was accused in a Jesuit thesis of appropriating other men's experiments without acknowledgement[68], he should have felt resentment, nor that his prejudices should have deepened.

The question was still the nature of a vacuum. Pascal wanted to establish, by incontrovertible proof, Torricelli's brilliant conjecture that the suspension of mercury in the barometer tube was due to atmospheric pressure. He did so with that elaboration and disregard of cost to which I referred last week. His experiments were begun at Rouen and continued in Paris[69], but the real triumph was achieved on the Puy-de-Dôme, 19 September 1648, when, the column of mercury falling steadily as the tube was carried up hill, the scholastic theory of Nature's horror of a vacuum was proved to be mere moonshine. In Pascal's record of the experiment he is scrupulous not to claim more than his due. He desires to assign to Galileo and Torricelli their proper share in the discovery of the new law; he is conscious of having lifted the veil some inches higher than either of them, and he is proud to have done so; but he is ready to rejoice with anyone who, using his conclusions, does yet more for science and for truth[70]. His success aroused sundry jealousies; Descartes, who might have known better, complained that *he* ought to have been mentioned, since he had urged the experiment on young Pascal against his will[71]. The Jesuits, as we have seen, called him a purloiner. Pascal's protest in reply to them is a model of dignity and candour. "No one is obliged to be learned any more than he is obliged to be rich; but no one is dispensed from the obligation of being sincere. The charge of ignorance or of indigence only hurts him who brings it. But that of theft is so heavy that no man of honour can see himself accused of it without the risk of his silence passing for a confession of guilt[72]." Here is the love of truth; here is also the point of honour. Two qualities which we have claimed for Pascal are proved, as he would have wished them proved, by special observation.

Between the experiment on the vacuum and his next scientific excursion there intervened the *Provincial Letters,* which must be treated separately. A word must be said now about the wrangle over the cycloid, which belongs to Pascal's last years. His discoveries in connexion with this curve mark his final effort in geometry.

Once more it is a question of priority, and here it must be admitted that at first sight Pascal seems to have been less than fair to his great predecessor Torricelli, and to deserve the harsh things which historians of mathematics have said of him[73]. But while allowing his unfairness we must observe that it was exhibited in behalf of a friend.

The cycloid and its properties had engaged the attention of a whole generation of mathematicians—Galileo and Torricelli in Italy, Mersenne and Roberval in France. Roberval, Pascal's senior by twenty years and a vain and irascible man, violently disputed first right in the solution of the area of the cycloid which Torricelli claimed for Galileo and himself. His insistence wore Torricelli down and extorted a weary letter saying that it did not matter whether the problem was solved in France or Italy, and that since Roberval was so jealous of the discovery, he was welcome to it[74]. Roberval seized upon this as a confession of defeat, and Pascal, taught by him, took it as such. There seems little doubt that between them they were unjust to Torricelli's memory. But there seems equally little doubt that Pascal's error was one of judgment solely, and that if a dupe, he was the dupe of his friendship[75].

On the other hand he is fighting for himself in the controversy with the Jesuit Lalouvère and our own countryman, Wallis. Having settled the quadrature of the cycloid, under the circumstances described last Sunday, he issued in June 1658 a challenge, as was the custom in the seventeenth century, with a prize of sixty *pistoles*[76] for a satisfactory solution of certain problems within three months. There was a large field of competitors, among them being Huygens and Christopher Wren; but Lalouvère and Wallis were the only two who claimed with any persistence to have satisfied the conditions. Pascal rode roughshod over their pretensions; but there is good modern authority[77] for believing that the judgment of his jury, if somewhat inelastic, was just; consequently he felt himself entitled to devote the *pistoles* to the printing of his own results. Lalouvère at least was quite incompetent; he hesitated and contradicted himself; he was guilty of the unforgivable in mathematics —he could not verify his own miscalculations[78]. In this affair, as always, Pascal is imperious and impatient, but he is strictly honest.

From this brief selection from his mathematical controversies we gather that Pascal had no reason to be pleased with Jesuit science. He was still less pleased with Jesuit doctrine and religious practice, and it is to this ground that he now invites us.

The quarrel between the Jansenists and the Jesuits, apart from the note of personal or professional jealousy which not infrequently dominates it[79], is but one incident in the long warfare that once raged round the problem of Free Will and Grace. That controversy is now laid to rest; we divide to-day on other questions, we utter other slogans; but, touching, as it does, the deepest things in philosophy and the very heart of religion, it may revive at any moment, and we should be ready for it. Pascal is one of those who will help us.

In the ultimate resort it is the old struggle between St Paul and Stoicism, between St Augustine and Pelagius. In the form under which it broke out a generation before Pascal it is the principles of the Reformation *versus* Scholasticism. The first home of Jansenism (for there were Jansenists before Jansénius) was Louvain—a name that cannot be heard to-day without emotion. During the first half of the sixteenth century Louvain was a fortress against Luther[80] and his doctrines of Grace and Predestination. The German reformer did not mince words in describing his opponents. Among the *Sauteologen, Sophisten, grobe Esel* of Louvain[81], as he elegantly terms them, was a young student, Michel De Bay, known in history as Baius. Setting out to read Luther and behind Luther in order to refute him, he became insensibly influenced by his views, and these he sedulously propagated in the University of which, in spite of repeated Papal censure, he died the honoured Chancellor in 1589[82]. His teaching brought him into violent conflict with the Jesuits. Louvain rang with the names of *Lutherani* and

Massilienses, and the pulpits echoed the invective of the streets[83]. The Baianists strengthened their position by founding, the year before their leader died, a special professorship for the confutation of the Jesuits[84]. Its first occupant was Jacques Janson, master and friend of Cornelius Jansen, afterwards bishop of Ypres, who in his turn succeeded to the chair and was soon engaged upon the mighty tome which supplied ammunition for his friends and foes alike. The *Augustinus* appeared at Louvain in 1640, two years after its author's death. It was the fruit of a prolonged intercourse with St Augustine, all of whose works Jansen had read through more than ten times, and those on the Pelagian writings no less than thirty times[85]. Its object was to reassert Augustine's doctrine on Grace against the Pelagianism and Semi-Pelagianism which threatened the Church. The Jesuits said that it was an attempt to throw the protection of the great doctor's name over the heresies of Baius, and they did their utmost to prevent its publication. In this they failed, but they succeeded in procuring a condemnation in general terms from Urban VIII in 1642[86].

The supporters of the book were dubbed Jansenists by their enemies, but they called themselves Augustinians, claiming, as was indeed the fact, that there was nothing between its covers which had not the support of the bishop of Hippo. They were vehemently incensed against the Spanish Jesuit Molina who had taken Augustine's name in vain[87], and they accused his followers, the Molinists, of reviving the heresies which the saint had laid low, of undermining the Faith in general and the article of Grace in particular, and of bartering away purity of doctrine and of morals for the sake of worldly success[88].

The mantles both of Jansen, who had chiefly combated the doctrine of the Molinists, and of his lieutenant Saint-Cyran, who impugned their moral discipline, descended on Antoine Arnauld, brother of *la Mère Angélique*, and the most conspicuous theologian connected with Port-Royal. His shoulders were broad enough for both, and the long row of his writings in forty-three volumes is a proof of it. The first of these was the tract *On Frequent Communion* (1643) which together with its sequel, entitled *The Moral Theology of the Jesuits*, form a fitting introduction to a long life of sincere devotion to controversy[89].

The immediate occasion of the tract was trivial enough. Two fashionable ladies[90] wanted to go to a ball. One of them, who had taken the Communion that same morning, was refused permission by her Jansenist confessor. The other carried the matter to her confessor, a Jesuit, who set out his views in a pamphlet. Arnauld, prompted by Saint-Cyran, refuted them. His reply, the *Frequent Communion*, must always be borne in mind when we read Pascal's handling of Jesuit precept and practice. Henceforward Arnauld, both for his own sake and his father's[91], is the special object of Jesuit attack and the willing champion of the *Augustinus*, both in the preliminary skirmishes and in the real battle which centres round the famous Propositions.

In 1649 five points of heresy, denying the Universality of Grace and Redemption, were discovered in the book, denounced to the Pope, and in due course, that is after long delay, condemned by him. It may be stated at once that with the exception of the first, all the Propositions were heretical in a constructive sense. They were inferences from what the Jesuits believed to be the teaching of the book. And even the first, though expressed in Jansen's words, was torn from a context which as Arnauld pointed out gave it a very different colour[92]. With regard to the other four, most people are content to echo Bossuet's dictum that they are the very soul of the book[93], without consulting the book itself. As a matter of fact, although it doubtless contains many passages which resemble the propositions, it also contains many which contradict them flatly, and it is quite as easy to miss them as to find them in its pages. It depends on the prejudice with which you set out to read it. What is certain is that Jansen had no intention of writing or quoting anything that favoured Calvinism, and further that any Calvinistic tendency betrayed by him comes in the last resort from his master St Augustine, whose privilege or fate it has been to furnish views to all the schools of Christianity in turn.

The Bull was accepted in France and both sides agreed to an armistice, from which Arnauld we may believe was not loth to be released by the provocative attitude and action of the Molinists. Things came to a head when a friend was refused absolution on account of his Jansenist tendencies[94]. Arnauld wrote two letters[95], one of 200 pages, to the Duc de Liancourt, the friend in question, the other to the Duc de Luynes, who was also of his party. Two passages were at once fastened upon. The first was the statement that the Propositions had been invented by the enemy and were not contained in the *Augustinus*; the other was a quotation from St Augustine to the effect that the Grace necessary to good works might fail a saint, and had in fact failed St Peter when he denied his Lord[96]. In other words

Arnauld was renewing the first Proposition which had been condemned as heretical. He was arraigned for temerity *de iure* and *de facto* before the Faculty of Theology of which he was doctor. This was at the end of 1655. The Sorbonne, sitting the whole of every morning, took six weeks to consider the question of fact—whether the Propositions were in *Augustinus.* Arnauld from the depth of Port-Royal wrote letter after letter, protesting his orthodoxy, condemning the Propositions wherever they might be found, expressing regret for his utterances. All in vain. On January 14, 1656, he was condemned on the point of fact—his justification of Jansen—and the Sorbonne addressed itself to the point of doctrine—the passage concerning St Peter's fall.

It was evident that the accused would fare no better on this count than he had on the other. The Dominicans or Thomists in the Sorbonne, who were inclined to leniency, were overruled by the Molinists[97]; a special new form of closure was invented—half an hour for each speaker by the sand-glass. Port-Royal was in despair. "You cannot let yourself be condemned like a child without telling the facts to the public," they cried. Arnauld was not what we call a popular writer—his genius did not lie that way—but he made an heroic effort. There are few more touching pictures than that of the redoutable dogmatic theologian coming down to his friends and reading to them the tract with which he meant to win the great heart of the people. Their evident disappointment infected him. "I see you do not think this letter any good," he says sadly, "and I believe you are right." But his failure led him straight to unhoped-for success. Turning suddenly to Pascal who was there with the rest, he said, "You who are young—

you ought to do something." It was explained to Pascal what was wanted. The public must be told simply and plainly that, whereas ostensibly the doctrine of Grace was at stake, it was really only a question of doubtful terms, a piece of theological phraseology. Was Arnauld to be branded as heretic because he had not said that Peter after his fall still possessed the "proximate power" of doing right[98]?

Pascal thought he could sketch something which the others could pull into shape. But when after a few days he submitted what he had written, they cried "That is excellent! that will do! we must have it printed." Printed it was, and published on 23 January 1656 in pamphlet form—eight quarto pages—under the title *Lettre escrite à un Provincial par un de ses amis sur le sujet des disputes présentes de la Sorbonne.* It was followed at short intervals by seventeen more, the last bearing date March 24, 1657. A nineteenth was begun, but it ends in the middle of a sentence on the second page. The Letters did not secure Arnauld, but they won for Pascal an immediate and immense controversial and literary success.

Did he deserve his triumph? Was he competent for the task laid upon him? He was not a professed student of theology. But he knew what Grace was; he had been granted something which he felt by nature he had not, and could not have. He knew Port-Royal and he loved his friends. So, trusting to them largely for his facts, he enters into the fray.

There were two questions before him; the nature of the Jesuit attack on Arnauld, and the character of Jesuit morality. He soon found that the second was the more important and to it he devotes twelve out of his eighteen letters. Only the first four and the last two deal with the case before the Sorbonne; from the eleventh onwards he drops his imaginary country correspondent and addresses the Jesuits directly. But before we consider his performance we must ourselves understand what really lay behind the verbal quibbles which he withers with the fire of his wit and sarcasm. Did his friends explain to him the differences, the great and the subtle differences which divided their foes from them and their foes among themselves? *We* must at least be clear on this point, and I will attempt a very brief statement of the various Grace doctrines of the rival parties.

The Jansenists, starting from a very exalted view of the perfection of man's nature before the Fall, held a proportionately low view of his condition after that event. All that rendered him acceptable to God, good in God's sight, was swept away when he lost the First Grace. The Fall entirely undid him, enslaved his will, rendering it an easy prey to the *delectatio terrena* and incapable of choosing the good. Left to himself, man goes down swiftly to eternal ruin. But God does not thus abandon him. He sends His Son to redeem him—or at least a restricted number of predestinate souls—and with His Son He bestows a free gift, His Grace, which touches the torpid will with a *delectatio caelestis*, conquers the *delectatio terrena*, inclines man to good instead of evil, and is infallibly efficacious for God's great purpose, viz. the salvation of His chosen. This efficacious Grace is irresistible, but God may withdraw it as He has bestowed it, without the play of human will; and when it is withdrawn, the man who had it once is in no better case than if he had never had it. He is once more helpless, hopeless, incapable of good[99].

Against the uncompromising logic of this scheme Dominican and Jesuit agreed to sink their ancient differences and maintain a doctrine which secured more room for the action of man's will and promised more hope for his future. To them the contrast between man's fallen and his innocent nature was not so sharp as Jansen found it. Man is still largely the arbiter of his own happiness. His will was weakened, damaged by the Fall, but not enslaved. And to assist it God sends a divine help, a Grace, which both agree in calling sufficient. At this point the differences begin. The Dominicans held that sufficient Grace was only sufficient to set free the will, illuminate it as to right and wrong, and incline it to good action. It was not sufficient to win heaven. What rewards await it may be left to God. This sufficient Grace is bestowed on all. Upon a select few, predestinate, God bestows a second Grace, which is more than sufficient, which is efficacious and irresistible. And even when God withdraws it, as He may, it leaves its traces. Man is not the same after it as he was before. There is left to him a proximate power of obeying God's commandments, a power which it is within his will to use right or wrong—a power real, though incomplete[100].

The Jesuits allow still greater scope to man's will. Like the Dominicans they admit a preliminary, sufficient Grace—sufficient not to save but to secure by prayer and by good works the second, efficacious Grace. The right use of sufficient Grace brings with it, as cause produces effect, efficacious Grace, which accordingly is efficacious not of itself alone but through the cooperation of man's will. It depends on man whether the sufficient Grace draws down efficacious Grace. If that efficacious Grace is withdrawn, a proximate power is still left, capable of inducing a fresh bestowal of efficacious Grace. In every case man's will plays a prominent and principal part[101].

It is plain that Jansenists and Molinists held extreme and opposite views. Midway between them stood the Dominicans, touching the Jansenists on the one hand in respect of the divinely arbitrary nature of efficacious Grace, and touching the Jesuits on the other hand in respect of the preliminary, sufficient Grace. They differed from the Jansenists in that their preliminary Grace set the will free; they differed from the Jesuits in their view of the process by which sufficient Grace was supplemented by efficacious Grace.

Middle parties are always open to the efforts of the extremes to win them to their side, and the long-standing quarrel between the Dominicans and the Jesuits as to the exact nature of the will and the part it played, encouraged the Jansenists to make the most of the resemblances between the Dominican system and their own. The practical policy of the Jansenists was to detach the Dominicans from the Jesuits. This is what Pascal attempts in his first two Letters. He has to shew that Dominican and Jesuit are agreed on a merely verbal compromise, measuring orthodoxy by a term "proximate power" which each of them interprets in his own way. When the Dominicans said that the just man had the proximate power of obeying the commandments they meant that nothing was wanting on his part. A man in a dark room has the proximate power of sight and will see when light comes. The Jesuits regarded proximate power as a reality; a man in a dark room has no proximate power of seeing. Pascal, the geometrician, has little difficulty in demolishing the flimsy structure of a charge founded on a mere equivocation[102].

In his Second Letter he deals with another equivocal term—Sufficient Grace. He establishes the essential agreement in the views of the Jansenists and the Dominicans in regard to the efficacy of a sufficient Grace, and exhibits the inconsistency of the Jesuit view, which is fatally attracting the Dominicans, that sufficient Grace needs a further Grace to make it efficacious, so that Grace is at once sufficient and not sufficient—which is absurd[103].

Before the Third Letter was written, Arnauld had been condemned on the point of faith. Pascal comments on the censure. It is a personal victory—the victory of divines and not of divinity. "We who are not doctors are unconcerned in their quarrels[104]." And with that he leaves the Dominicans.

The Fourth Letter brings us upon other ground. Pascal passes from the periphery to the centre. It is no longer a question of cleverly indicating points of contact and angles of divergence, but of revealing a fundamental cleavage between views of human responsibility. The Jesuit, looking chiefly at the sinful act, made knowledge and will the measure of its guilt. The less the consciousness of sin in committing the sinful act, the less the responsibility of the agent. The further the state in which the act is done lies outside the will's control—ignorance, thoughtlessness, passion—the better claim has the man to be freed from imputation. The single act is torn away from its context of preceding actions, thoughts, habits, which go to make up character. Now it is precisely character, rather than will and knowledge, that engaged the attention of the Jansenists. We are not merely wills, we are natures—and corrupted natures—and from the poisoned springs of our nature sinful thoughts and words and acts are constantly welling up[105]. They are ours—we cannot escape responsibility for them. The "secret faults" of the psalmist are as real and as really ours as wilful, conscious sins. The Jesuit view is set forth through the medium of the *dramatis persona*, one of their fashionable directors: and from this point onwards for twelve letters it is to Jesuit direction of the conscience and its results that Pascal confines himself. Why? Because it was a more popular subject? To win a *succès de scandale*? So it was hinted, and that the Chevalier de Méré put him up to the move[106]. Port-Royal was sorry that he abandoned Grace, and so may we be, for we have now to piece together from the *Pensées* what otherwise would have stood out clear in the light of his telling logic and his dazzling wit. But the fact is that he had begun to read Escobar and the Casuists and felt a call to deal with them, which he does very faithfully. He did not let himself be hurried. None of his Letters, except perhaps the first two, are thrown off at white heat[107]. One of them (no. XVIII) he rewrote thirteen times; of another (no. XVI) he says "I had not time to make it shorter[108]"—a plea which lecturers and preachers may sometimes be suffered to put in.

Casuistry was not the invention of the Jesuits. Wherever troubled consciences seek counsel upon doubtful points, there must be casuists and casuistry. And the list of those who have written on the subject, Jews,

Latins, Fathers, Schoolmen, Reformers, Puritans, is as honourable as any in civilisation. No member of the University of William Perkins, Joseph Hall, and Jeremy Taylor, will cast a stone at the Casuists. But the Jesuits put their own seal upon casuistry and used it, not to make things difficult for the penitent, but as easy as was consistent with rules of Christian conduct. I do not say principles, but rules. For whereas casuists of the Reformed Churches always referred in the last resort to the tribunal of Scripture, the Jesuits, going less far afield, were content with the decision of any grave doctor[109]. Such a decision may be regarded as having a fair amount of Probability and may be safely followed, even though our own heart condemn us.

Of grave doctors holding different views there has never been a lack; and many of them had published books which, though doubtless intended first as manuals for confessors, attained by their wide circulation a very much more popular character. Pascal for instance works upon the thirty-sixth edition of Escobar's *Theologia Moralis*. Bauny's *Somme des péchés* had a vogue corresponding to the attractiveness of its title, while Busenbaum's *Medulla* has been reprinted fifty times.

The doctrine of Probabilism, which is the inevitable consequence of a compulsory confessional and a multitude of confessors, the germ of which appears as soon as books of penitence began to be written[110], flourished especially in the later middle ages and was eagerly adopted by the Society of Jesus. It suited their object, which was to conduct as many souls by as many paths as possible to heaven. "When," wrote Escobar, "I see so many different opinions in Christian morality, I am conscious of the clear shining of divine providence, for amid this variety of opinions, the yoke of Jesus Christ is easier to bear. Is it not better for a gentleman who has to go from Valladolid to Madrid to be shewn several roads, than if there were only one? For that one must either be too broad, or impeded by the multitude of wayfarers, and it would be difficult to walk in[111]."

Pascal knew of but one way and that a narrow one. And before this multiplication of facile means to salvation, his whole soul rose in wrath. Is it conceivable that, conscious of the great danger, he should have paused to consider whether the cases cited by Escobar and Bauny were only meant for the eye of the priest in confession, "only subtle or eccentric speculations of divines[112]"? The books were poisonous to him; they breathed a flame which must be stamped out. So, taking his cue from Arnauld, he goes pencil in hand through Escobar, notes each extravagant or outrageous case, holds it up to scorn, shews how this collection of possible or impossible human weaknesses suggests the sins it would correct and empties the Gospel of its comfort. And the Letters continue *rinforzando*. In the Sixteenth he works back again to Port-Royal and its suffering saints, and in the Seventeenth and Eighteenth to Arnauld. These last two contain a special problem and must be left for the moment. Our present duty is to consider whether his attack was justified, whether his method was honest.

It is generally assumed, at any rate by Protestant authors, that Pascal is fair in his handling of the Jesuit position but sometimes unfair in his details. I believe the converse to be true[113]. Pascal is fair, scrupulously fair, in his quotations from Jesuit writings, but unjust in his interpretation of Jesuit motives. He does not charge them with wilfully corrupting morals. That he distinctly says is not their design. But neither is it their object to reform morals. No, they think so well of themselves as to believe it to be beneficial and necessary for religion that they should extend their empire over all the earth and be the keepers of all consciences[114]. One is reminded of another more real and recent bid for world dominion founded on a similar excuse.

They were ambitious, magnificently ambitious, but not for themselves. Their motto was *Ad maiorem Dei gloriam*, and we need not deny them the credit of acting up to it. They had spent themselves for the Church; they had helped to raise it from the ruin of the religious wars; their services to education and learning were unrivalled; their missionary zeal was unbounded[115]. Their wonderful organisation, their genius for obedience, marked them out for empire, for the evangelisation of society. They were not afraid of the world and its contagion; they boldly said: *nihil humani a me alienum puto.* Sometimes the world caught and conquered them, or they compromised with it; in endeavouring to bring religion within the reach of all, they lowered it; the sharp sword lost its edge in their hands; they put cushions under the knees of the penitent.

Pascal and his friends saw only this, the weak side of the Order, and missed its greatness, its high aims, its noble achievement. Holding a radically different view of man, seeing in him a damaged nature, incapable of good, perfectibility to them was an illusion, progress a false light, the apostles of progress false leaders. They refused to find in them any good at all. There might have been good at the beginning, but the old tradition was forgotten or forgone.

All this was mistaken. For good or ill the policy of the Jesuits had never changed. Personal piety, personal holiness was still the purpose of their noviciate, the winning of the world to Christ the object of their warfare. Doubtless the Jesuits of Pascal's day were, man for man, not comparable to the saints and scholars who adorned the Order, say under Aquaviva, a generation before. There is no name among them that can be set beside Ribadeneira, Maldonatus, Bellarmine, Cornelius à Lapide. Pascal's antagonists are *epigoni*. In France, no doubt, the atmosphere of the Court had corrupted the original purity of their ambition, their obedience, and their faith; from Father Coton, confessor to Henri IV, onwards the keepers of the royal conscience were all Jesuits. But Pascal is not primarily concerned with individuals but with a system which has never changed its principles since the day when it was first started until now[116]; and he was historically wrong in his attack. Yet we cannot but hold that his instinct was sound and his victory deserved.

Dr Hort somewhere warns us against the reckless use of legal phraseology in spiritual things[117], and laments the injury wrought in the Church thereby. Legal phraseology is the expression of the juridical mind; and that is what was wrong with the Jesuits and what Pascal would set right. They were judges, but complaisant judges. They thought they could give infallible rules whereby to gauge the amount of sin involved in a particular act. To Pascal's mind no human science can distinguish between the wrong that a man does and the wrong that he is.

They thought that the cases dealt with by their grave doctors sufficiently prescribed the penitence necessary for securing absolution. Pascal, feeling himself to be when his best is done but an unprofitable servant, will not measure the how much and the how little. They knew the attractive power of the comfortable words, "Come unto me"; but they forgot the sequel. Not only, not chiefly the travailing and the heavy laden were summoned by them to bear the easy yoke, made easier by their rules, but willing bearers of worldly burdens. Pascal remembers another sterner summons: "Take up the cross and follow me." And we who are so busy making religion pleasant and inviting, though we should cry out at the thought of standing in his pillory beside the Jesuits, we feel as we hear him, that he reproaches us also. Maybe his words, chastising compromise and softness, will come home to hearts where the iron has deeply entered in, which the sword is piercing as it does ours to-day. But the serious call must issue from lips which we believe have been touched by the coal from off the altar, or men will not listen. And only when we know that it was in his zeal for truth that Pascal shewed so little mercy to his opponents can we forgive his misreading of their motives.

There remains a word to be said about the two final *Provincial Letters* which join the first four of the series on the one hand, and on the other the breach with Port-Royal already mentioned. In Letter XVII Pascal returns to Arnauld's case, and to the distinction between the *question de fait* and the *question de droit* which he had in his first Letter raised and dropped. He is now speaking straight to the Père Annat, Confessor to the King,

Provincial of the Order, always a most strenuous opponent of Jansenism and, it would appear, the chief draughtsman of the Formulary of 1656, which you will remember demanded signature respecting the Five Propositions.

It is usually said that these last two Letters shew a loss of cunning in Pascal's hand, that they stir a conflict on a point of petty interest. We shall not admit this if we read them and their sequel, the Note on the Signature, with any intelligence of the Roman Catholic mind and position, and see what they disclose, the picture of Pascal struggling first between loyalty to Rome and loyalty to his friends, and then between loyalty to Rome and loyalty to Truth. The point at issue is not small. It is nothing less than the question of Papal Infallibility. Indeed the distinction between fact and doctrine, *fait et droit*, is a distinction which those who support Infallibility must admit. Take an instance from early history. When Pope Zosimus in the fifth century first acquitted Pelagius and Caelestius of heresy and then at the instance of the African bishops condemned them, the only possible excuse for him under the theory of Infallibility is that his doctrine was sound all through and that he only went wrong on the question of fact, viz. whether Pelagius and Caelestius had contravened it[118]. Nor is the distinction without its effect on recent action. May it not be that when Pius X condemned Modernism, "the synthesis of all the heresies," he had in mind the old difficulties and quarrels about fact and doctrine, and that to avoid rekindling them, he made no mention of the authors of error when he gave sentence on the error itself[119]? So the distinction between *fait* and *droit* is of living interest and is still arguable.

And Pascal argues it with his wonted *maestria* and with convincing illustration. Pope and Church are infallible on points of doctrine, but not on points of fact. Witness Pope Zachary who threatened belief in the Antipodes with excommunication; witness Rome's recent decree against Galileo's opinion concerning the earth's motion. "That will never prove that it stands still; and if men had some observations which proved it is the earth which turns, not all mankind together would prevent its turning, nor prevent their turning with it[120]." This stroke surely shews no loss of power. It is the lion's claw. Yet we find him in 1661 going back on what he had written in 1656, and declaring in a memorandum on the projected subscription to the Formulary that doctrine and fact are so mixed up in this document as to be practically inextricable. "I condemn the Five Propositions in the sense of Jansen, or the doctrine of Jansen on the Five Propositions."

The point had been referred by Port-Royal to a good friend, the Bishop of Alet, and he had also, independently, given as his opinion that on this occasion the two questions of fact and doctrine were inseparable, and he advised, for the sake of prudence and unity, that they should sign the Formulary. Pascal comes to the same conclusion, but in the interest of truth and out of loyalty to the doctrine of Grace, he advises that they should not sign it. Is there anything false or dishonest in this contradiction of a former view? I do not think so. He still believes and he still asserts that the two things are separable in theory. They ought to be treated apart. But what is true in theory is sometimes impossible in practice, if truth is really to be maintained and the conscience kept clear in the matter of Grace. Their separability may be argued in a fly-sheet (*écrit volant*), but when it comes to signing a document which expressly condemns both together, the responsibility is too great to admit of any action which may be misinterpreted. The fly-sheets with their clever pleading on a subtle point will perish—the signatures appended to the Formulary condemning Jansen will remain[121]. So he bids the nuns be firm and refuse their names.

It was no light decision. It meant much for him. He had no desire to shake off allegiance to Rome. In the seventeenth *Provincial Letter* he had declared his belief that outside communion with the Pope, the sovran head of the Church, there is no salvation, and in a private letter of the same date he had written, "I will never sever myself from his communion[122]." Yet now he is ready himself, and he advises those he loves, to defy the Pope. Here is devotion to the Truth, if ever was. Here, as always, Pascal, when he sees it, is prepared to sacrifice all for Truth.

Such was Pascal in Controversy. I trust and hope I have not been unfair to him or his opponents, and that the time we have spent on what are after all the approaches and external circumstances of my subject has not been lost. It would, I think, have been a mockery to open the book of his heart and read there things about God and the Soul, Sin and Grace, as deep as have been written since the days of Christ's Apostles, if at the back of our mind we had the feeling that Pascal, who saw in the contemplation of the divine Mercy and Truth the cure for pride and sloth, twin sources of our sins, had himself wilfully fallen short of his ideal and had been disobedient to the heavenly vision.

III

O the depth of the riches both of the wisdom and the knowledge of God! how unsearchable are his judgements, and his ways past finding out! Romans xi. 33.

In announcing these lectures last term I stated that, after dealing with some points in Pascal's biography and considering his conduct of controversy, I should in my third and fourth lectures treat of his doctrinal system and his personal religion; out of which there will naturally arise some general remarks about the present value of his teaching and example.

Now the main source upon which we have to draw for a knowledge of his doctrinal system is the volume that passes under the name of his *Pensées*, perhaps the most unsystematic book ever printed. Its history is briefly this. When Pascal died, in August 1662, several bundles of papers in all shapes and sizes were found in his room, covered with disjointed and often scarcely legible notes and reflexions upon topics religious, philosophical, and critical. These were put into a sort of order by his friends and his family, and a selection of them published, not without some little embellishments and arrangements[123], as soon as it was safe to do so. That seemed to be in 1668, when the Pope, Clement IX, declaring himself contented with signature to the Formulary condemning the Five Propositions so far as regarded doctrine and with respectful silence on the question of fact, established the Peace of the Church—a peace which was but a truce and did not prevent the ruthless repression of Port-Royal thirty years later[124].

Accordingly in 1670 appeared the *Pensées de M. Pascal sur la religion et sur quelques autres sujets* with a preface by his nephew Etienne Perier. This is known as the edition of Port-Royal. There have been innumerable other editions in widely different arrangements according to the taste of successive editors. To mention the chief, there was in the eighteenth century what may be termed the philosophical edition, more complete but more sophisticated than that of Port-Royal, which we owe to the combined talent of Condorcet and Voltaire, who contributed notes of pungent criticism and somewhat patronizing praise. Three years afterwards, in 1779, came the Abbé Bossut, who knocked out the philosophical commentary and enabled the waning century to read Pascal apart from any disturbing medium. In 1835 M. Frantin attempted to recover the original order and the Christian intention of the *Thoughts.* But there was good ground for the appeal which Victor Cousin made to the French Academy in 1845. He called loudly for a return to the autograph MS languishing in the Royal Library and for the production of an honest text, free from the substitutions and suppressions, the changes of thought and expression which early editors had dared to introduce. The challenge was taken up by M. Faugère, who unfortunately did not go to the autograph MS, but worked from a private copy in his own possession, which was patently defective. In 1851 Ernest Havet rendered great service by a commentary and exposition of the *Pensées* which no student can afford to neglect. But he left the critical problem untouched, and it was not until 1877 that Faugère's error was in any way rectified. In that year Auguste Molinier produced a very beautiful book, founded on the original MS, and noteworthy among other points for its adherence to Pascal's orthography. Then in 1897 M. Léon Brunschvicg printed all the fragments in an edition which is at once the handiest and cheapest and which he reissued in more sumptuous form in 1908[125].

All these editions have classified the fragments according to their elective affinities, grouping them in the order which recommended itself to the respective editors. And it is still open to any one to make a new arrangement for himself. For this there is full material. Professor Michaut of Fribourg has had the happy idea, which seems to have suggested itself to no one before, of publishing the *Pensées* in the order of the original MS, with a complete critical apparatus; and quite recently M. Brunschvicg has crowned his services in the cause of Pascal by giving us a photographic facsimile of the precious documents, in which the reader can follow the varying moods of the writer, and observe how the character of the handwriting corresponds to the movements of his mind[126].

But under whatever form the *Pensées* are presented to us, inasmuch as the MS was left by Pascal a mass of disorder, they suggest anything rather than a system. Yet Pascal had his system and we have a double record of it. One, rather dry and dignified, from the pen of his nephew; the other picturesque and living, but nevertheless equally or, in virtue of its life and movement, even more trustworthy, by Filleau de la Chaise, who was a member of the little committee charged with the sorting of the papers, and who was not so well treated as he deserved by the others[127]. We are fortunate in having him to go to for an account of the memorable occasion when Pascal unfolded his plan. We must not however invoke his help until we have heard what Pascal said to his confessor only six weeks before his death.

In that conversation to which I have already made reference with Father Beurrier, *curé* of his parish, St Étienne-du-Mont, the dying man declared that "for the last two years he had withdrawn from the great dispute about Grace and Predestination and had been thinking of his own salvation and how to combat the ungodly and the atheists then abounding in Paris, as well as the regular heretics; he had already collected materials and weapons most potent to convince them of the truth of the Catholic religion; he knew by experience their strong and their weak points, having in time past conversed and conferred with the most stubborn among them; they believed in him, and he knew how to handle them and convince them; the materials he spoke of were diverse thoughts, arguments, and reasons which he had written down in a few words, at different times and without any order, but just as he formed them in his mind, in the purpose which he had of making a book of them, setting them out in order and explaining them very clearly, and giving them all the force he could; he hoped that this book would be very useful and that God would bless it, seeing the purity of his intention, which was nothing else than to win back these straying sheep to the fold of the Church and thus extend the kingdom of Jesus Christ and procure God's glory and the salvation of men's souls. It was for this purpose alone that he wanted health and longer life, if such were God's will, whom he prayed to move men of learning and honesty to leave the wretched quarrels that divided them and join with him in a common effort against infidelity and heresy[128]."

There are one or two things to remark in this important passage which has only quite recently been recovered for us. The first is the plain statement of his purpose. He wanted to confute atheism, to persuade the *libertins* or freethinkers. The other is the value to him of that worldly experience with which we were engaged for so long last term. He knew these men at first hand; he had their ear. One small point needs a note of elucidation. Madame Perier, in the *Life* of her brother, tells us that what suggested the Apology for Christianity to him was the miracle of the Holy Thorn in March 1656, when her little daughter Margot was cured of a lachrymal abscess by the application of a relic from Christ's Crown[129].

The truth seems rather to be that the miracle precipitated an intention which had been floating in Pascal's mind ever since his second conversion in 1654. This does not really clash with his statements to Beurrier, first, that he had written down his thoughts at different times, and later, that he had been writing them down during the past two years. His custom was to form and carry in his head whatever he meant to write and to use no notebook. So tenacious was his memory that, as he himself said, he never forgot anything he wanted to remember[130]. He kept his ideas locked up until they were mature and then he wrote. He rewrote, as we know, sometimes a dozen times; but that is different from writing by the aid of notes. And the fact is that if death had taken him in the fulness of his bodily power we should have had no fragments even. But when his ailments gathered on him and his memory began to fail and he had not strength to retain the flashes of his intuition, he adopted as a habit and to relieve his overburdened mind what he had hitherto only done haphazard, and wrote down all his thoughts as they came to him, in a few words and sometimes in half words. But all the time he had his plan, and to it and the account of its development before his friends we now return.

Filleau de la Chaise, who tells the story of what took place in 1657 or 1659 (I incline to the later date), vividly recalls how they all sat enthralled for two hours or more while Pascal shaped his design with his incomparable logic, and fixed it with the fire of his eloquence[131].

After first sweeping aside the proofs men ordinarily use, the ontological and the metaphysical, as unsatisfying, these to man's heart and those to his intelligence, he declared that only proofs moral and historical would serve, and that they must be such as will appeal to natural feeling and personal experience. Here was at once a surprise and, we may guess, a disappointment for his hearers. They would have welcomed, being all worshippers of mathematics, a proof of the existence of God and of the immortality of the soul, conducted on geometrical principles, leading on from proposition to proposition to the final demonstration. Or they looked for a piece of abstract reasoning, for most of them were metaphysically-minded.

What Pascal, rejecting the unilinear method, promises to give them is "a cumulation of probabilities, independent of each other, arising out of the nature and circumstances of the case—probabilities too fine to avail separately, too subtle and circuitous to be convertible into syllogisms, too numerous and various for such conversion, even were they convertible[132]." Many of you, doubtless, recognize the passage. Newman's words in the *Grammar of Assent* fit themselves so exactly to what Pascal meant that I do not hesitate to adopt them. A mass of convergent proof which shall convince the ordinary man of the truth of Christianity by an intangible process like that which leads him to believe in the present existence of Rome, in the past existence of Mahomet, in the reality of the fire of London—that is what Pascal means to marshal in his *Apologia.*

He starts from facts most generally familiar, the facts of human nature. He takes a worldling—the Chevalier de Méré or Mitton—and forces him to look into the glass. It is not a pleasing vision. Never, says Filleau de la Chaise, did those who have most despised man (he has Montaigne in mind, and so no doubt had Pascal) lay such stress upon his imbecility, his corruption, and his darkness.

Pascal, then, begins by startling his friend. When he is thoroughly alarmed at what he sees, then and not till then will he shew him another picture—man's essential but long-forfeited beauty and nobility, his high thoughts, his hunger for goodness. The result produces hopeless perplexity. Each of us is an extravagant composite of incompatibles—the ineradicable love of truth joined with the utter incapacity for attaining it; the inextinguishable pride flaunting through the vileness and the misery; the dull sense that something is wanting, we know not what; the pricks of conscience even when we are at our best—all these contrarieties, this single multiple nature, make us wonder whether we are children of chance or whether it was God that made us so[133].

The man is genuinely disturbed and ready to enquire. To whom shall he go? Pascal sends him to the philosophers, and has little difficulty in convincing him that they have not the answer to the riddle, with their contradictions, their false assertions and conclusions. After philosophy, religion in its infinite varieties through the ages. Not one of these is able to move him. If there be a Governor of the universe who vouchsafes to reveal Himself, He must have a worship suited to Him and declare a doctrine worthy of Him. But as a fact what does this review disclose? Religions which begin and end with the race that practises them; religions in which gods many, and more ridiculous than man, are worshipped; religions devoid of spirituality or nobility, which sanction vice, which prevail by force or fraud, which lack all proof and authority, whose cults are gross and carnal, utterly unworthy of God, which tell nothing about God, and about man tell nothing but his extravagances.

The novice is on the point of despair and suicide, when Pascal shews him a better way[134]. He bids him turn his eyes upon a particular people, sprung from one authentic ancestor, keeping themselves with such care from contamination with other races that their story is practically the story of a single family and challenges comparisons with that of all others in point of antiquity and credibility. He shews him that this wonderful people finds its sanction and reads its history in a wonderful Book which by its unity and coherence compels belief. Moreover this Book contains the information which the freethinker has vainly sought elsewhere, and which satisfies the questionings of his mind and the craving of his heart. From it he learns that the order of nature which he cannot but admire is not due, as his Epicurean creed would have him think, to a fortuitous clash of atoms, but to the operation of one God; that man was not once the hopeless creature he is to-day, but a Being made as like to God as the finite can be to the infinite, gifted with intelligence and light, free of will and action, responsive to justice and reason, animated by the Spirit of the Perfect Mind which created him.

The man, for he is well read, perhaps remembers Longinus's definition of the Sublime, and finds that the Book answers thereto, speaking with exquisite simplicity and restraint. Only one who knew the truth could write like that. And yet—and yet—the contrast between what man is and what he is described as having been, raises the doubts which the beauty of the narrative had silenced[135]. Pascal turns to Genesis, ch. ii. That gift of Free-will was abused by man. His first use of it was to defy his Maker. Punishment was inevitable and proportionate to the sin. Death and ruin followed swiftly, with the loss of all his privileges and the withdrawal of God into impenetrable darkness. The only gleam of light left to him is an impotent desire to know; the only fragment of liberty, the liberty to sin. Thus he has become this incomprehensible portent which is called man, and he communicates his corruption to his children and his children's children, till he has peopled the world with wretches blind and criminal like himself.

From Genesis Pascal leads his willing learner on through the rest of the Old Testament, and shews him how every page echoes the corruption of man, the deceitfulness of the heart, repeats the horrors that man knows concerning himself, yes, and discovers fresh and unsuspected depths of degradation. But not only does this Book teach man more of himself than he knew before, and than any other book has done; it is the only one that speaks worthily of God and His inestimable majesty. It is the only one that teaches the love of God and puts the fulfilment of His Will as the great duty of all created things. Man is enabled to do his part through a God-given faculty of choice and love, which inclines him to offer himself a willing sacrifice.

This Book further solves the problems which have most teased pagan thinkers, such as the diversity that exists between men of the same common nature—differences of soul, of intelligence, of character, and the insane confusion that is in the world, leading philosophers to doubt of Providence. Why do the wicked almost always flourish while the just are miserable and downtrodden? Why this monstrous mixture of rich and poor, of tyrants and oppressors? Why are some born to happiness and others to suffering? Why all the errors, varieties of opinion, manners, and habits in the vast field of religion?

The first of these problems is accounted for by the doctrine of the Fall which enslaved the soul to the body, making it depend on accidents of birth, country, temperament, custom, having no right to affect an immortal essence. The second is solved by the bright hope of a better day in the life to come, when all anomalies will be reconciled, when the veil will be lifted which it has pleased God to draw for the sake of man's discipline.

Here is indeed a Book to awaken love and trust—the only book that, knowing human misery, promises remedy and brings present comfort. Man's case is not so desperate after all.

The freethinker mutters the word "illusion." Perhaps, says Pascal, but the thing is worth trying; the promises awaken hope; the remedy deserves to be tasted. And note, he continues, the crowning mercy. The remedy is not in our hands. If it were, we might well despair—our corrupt and feeble hands. But the Bible bids us look to God who will not fail, and who will send a Liberator to avert the wrath, repair the impotency, and render man capable of doing what is required of him[136]. The system, you must admit, is noble; it has the hall-mark of divinity[137]. Intuition and experience unite to tell us that these high thoughts are quite beyond anything that the human mind is capable of inventing.

The freethinker objects the unreasonableness and injustice of the doctrines of original sin and its transmission, and of the vicarious sufferer. Reason! cries Pascal. Be thankful that in a matter which concerns you so closely you are not at the sole mercy of reason which often fails us in judging trifles, and is not competent to decide on what is just or possible. We have *facts* which appeal to the simplest intelligence[138]. Here follow the arguments from miracles and prophecy, which Pascal himself regarded as most sovran for winning faith, and which, especially the latter, as he developed it, transported his hearers.

With regard to the first of these arguments we must

note the effect on Pascal's mind of the miracle of the Holy Thorn, which provided him with evidence so convincing that from thenceforth he took for his device an eye within a crown of thorns, and the words *scio cui credidi*. With regard to the latter, the modern reader will be content to remember that criticism was not yet born and that Richard Simon at this date was under twenty years of age[139].

The argument to which prophecy leads has for us a more attractive force—"the sinlessness of Jesus." If He had no prophecies or miracles, there is something so divine in His doctrine and His life, that one must at least be charmed by It, and admit that as His beauty wins our love so His greatness compels our admiration. Socrates and Epictetus pale before Him—human virtue is but a poor reflexion of the charity which He taught and was; true notions of justice come only to those who follow Him.

Such a Life as His is as great a miracle as to raise the dead or to transport mountains. None but God could have set such an ideal, none but God could have fulfilled it[140]. Does not the spectacle of this life remove your doubts? Or rather do not the doubts which remain arise from moral causes? If Jesus Christ were only offered to our eyes as a unique original and our hearts were not bidden copy Him, we should have no difficulty in confessing Him worthy of worship[141]. It is the *Imitatio Christi* that keeps us back. Then, soften the heart and let it have the scope to which it is entitled; so and only so the clouds will lift. Religion is not geometry. God's Truth does not shine upon the unjust and the just alike. There is much in nature that we do not understand; we only see a very little way; but we believe that the cause which we do not see must correspond to the effects which we do see, and we believe in its existence. Why not in religion trust the intuition which serves us so well in things of nature? Be reasonable within the limits of your understanding, and do not say 'impossible' and so make yourself ridiculous and miserable[142].

Such, in faint and broken outline, is the outline of Pascal's plan for his Apology, which was intended not to impart faith, nor to change the heart[143]—God alone can do that—but just to prove that there is no verity in the world better established than the truth of Christianity, and that man neglects it at his proper peril. Faint as it is, it discloses a definite system of thought, a regular system of doctrine, and if we have it in mind or in hand as we read the *Pensées*, we shall find that most of them fit into it and illustrate it. Not all of them indeed, and it is that which makes them such fascinating and perplexing reading. We cannot be sure that everything he jotted down was designed for future use; whether for instance the famous Wager-Essay[144], proving like an algebraical equation the ancient proposition that there is more profit in belief, was meant as a serious argument or whether it was a *tour de force*, a piece of mathematical virtuosity; we cannot always tell whether the cries of doubt and despair that strike our ear are his or his imaginary disputant's—"All men naturally hate one another." "Men are of necessity so mad that it would be madness of another kind not to be mad." "The last act is tragic, however brave the comedy before it; at the end a little earth is cast upon our head and all is over for ever[145]."

We do not know that the fragment which he called "the mystery of Jesus[146]," with its passionate adoration and its echoes of the divine Consoler's voice, was meant for any eyes but Pascal's, like the precious Memorial which he wore next his heart and which was found there at his death. We must always be exercising the judgement against which he warns us and the intuition which he extolled, as we turn the pages. But out of the confusion and uncertainty there emerges the figure of a mind and a heart working through darkness to the light, and having as guide the teaching of the Church as he had received it and as the circumstances of his stormy life conditioned it. It is of importance for us to see what his inheritance was and what modifications it underwent.

The point from which he set out is unquestionably Jansenism. That was inevitable.

Think of his life-story. Brought up by a father whose religion was marked by sanity rather than sanctity[147], this boy appears to have known no temptation to doubt, nor even to question. His precocity was for matters mathematical, not spiritual. The general conversion of the family to Jansenism at Rouen under the influence of the Rouvillistes did not prevent Blaise and his father from mixing with the world or from opposing the sister's withdrawal from it. For Blaise at least this first conversion was very like St Augustine's, touching the head rather than the heart[148]. He was in fact converted not so much to religion as to theology. The metaphysics of Jansenism, and especially its rigorous logic, satisfied him. He was, his sister tells us, always eager to know the reason of things; he had always a brightness of understanding to discern admirably well whatever was false from what was true. At all times and in all things truth alone was the object that he aimed at, since to find out truth was the sole satisfaction that he had. Wherefore from his tender infancy he could never be persuaded by anything that did not appear to him to be evidently true; so that when unsound reasons were given him, he would seek out others for himself, and when once he had attached himself to anything he could not quit it till he had found a reason which satisfied him[149]. Ah! the gallant little geometrician. And now at the age of twenty-three he met with a religion which proved itself mathematically, by $a + b$, logically, inexorably. Pascal leapt to it. He defends it publicly, and not without acrimony, against an ex-Capucin monk[150] who impugned it; he preaches it to his family—his private letters to his sisters at this time are nothing else than little sermons. Certainly he was an ardent Jansenist.

But both defence and letters are wanting in that fire, that mingled passion and tenderness, which are the mark of the Pascal whom we know and love. They are of the head, not from the heart. They are full of borrowed notions. Then came the second conversion at midnight on November 23, 1654, which wrought a real change in him. Jacqueline the nun tells us something of its outward results. No one but Pascal knew the inward truth, until next his heart, silent and cold in death, was found the piece of parchment upon which he had written in words of flame the record of his mystical rapture.

It is the Lord's Highpriestly prayer on the eve of His Passion that kindled the fire of Pascal's love and faith and loosened his tongue. The knowledge of the Father whom the world has not known, the God not of the philosopher and the wise man but of Abraham, Isaac, and Jacob, and the knowledge of Jesus Christ who reveals Him, bringing eternal life. This is the sum of the message borne in upon Pascal as he cons the seventeenth chapter of St John that sleepless night. It beats him down upon his knees in bitter grief for the sins which have kept him in darkness. "I have severed myself from Him; shunned Him, denied Him, crucified Him." It raises him to stand erect, conscious of his inherent dignity. "Greatness of the human soul." It sets free the springs of living waters which were sealed, and the fountains of his tears—tears of penitence and joy. It fills his heart with certainty, happiness, and peace; it thrills his deepest chords. "Certitude, Certitude. Feeling, Joy, Peace. Joy, joy, joy, tears of joy." Henceforth the Gospel, which has not now merely fallen on his ear but has reached his heart, shall be his only guide in the short passage through present troubles to eternal bliss. Earth and all save God are put away. "I will not forget thy word[151]." The whole curve of the progress towards the freedom of the sons of God, with its alternations of rise and fall, is traced in this page of broken utterance. The joy is mixed with trembling, but certainty prevails. Not the cool certainty of the intellect convinced by argument, but the touch with reality, the sense of actual presence of God within the heart.

This vision gives us the key that unlocks the *Pensées*. It is to the memory of that sacred night that we must assign all those passages which speak of the heart's answer to the call; for it was to the heart that God then spoke through the mind. Henceforth Pascal listens eagerly for its reasons; "the heart has its reasons which reason does not know." It is the heart which is conscious of God, not the reason. This then is Faith; God sensible to the heart, not to the reason. "Reason acts slowly and with so many views, on so many principles, which it must always keep before it, that it constantly slumbers and goes astray from not having its principles at hand. The heart does not act thus; it acts in a moment, and is always ready to act. We must then place our faith in the heart, or it will be always vacillating."

"We know truth, not only by the reason, but also by the heart, and it is from this last that we know first principles; and reason, which has nothing to do with it, tries in vain to combat them....Our knowledge of first principles, as space, time, motion, number, is as distinct as any principle derived from reason. And reason must lean necessarily on this instinctive knowledge of the heart, and must found thereon its every process[152]." Of course he keeps the form of doctrine he has received—the Jansenist system is maintained because, but only so far as, it accords with experience of the new life he has won and is winning. And when that experience widens, Pascal, both as a living Christian and as a man of science, admits new elements into his system of belief.

Now something happened two years later, in the middle of his *Provincial Letters*, which notably extended his outlook on the world and God's workings. He came into touch with a profounder and larger school of divinity, and he saw the travail of a human soul. He caught some glimpses of the teaching of St Thomas, and he watched a struggle between Nature and Grace.

You will remember that the main task of Port-Royal at the time of Arnauld's trial was to detach the Thomist or Dominican party, in the Sorbonne, from the Jesuit or Molinist, and to signalize the resemblances between Jansenism and the doctrine of Aquinas. Arnauld and Nicole were particularly bent on establishing these points of contact, and their policy dictated the earlier *Provincial Letters.* The point of resemblance was that both Jansenist and Thomist believed in a gift of Grace, necessary to salvation—gratuitous, irresistible, efficacious. The superficial difference was that whereas Jansen saw nothing but eternal ruin awaiting the man who was untouched by this sole Grace, or who having once been touched was abandoned by it, the Thomists posited an initial, general Grace, a sufficient Grace granted to all men, which prepares the heart for the infusion of the efficacious Grace. Further they would not surrender to eternal damnation the mass of men who were untouched or abandoned by efficacious Grace, but allowed a proximate power of accomplishing the divine commandments and of soliciting a fresh infusion of efficacious Grace[153].

A deeper difference was their view of the part which man plays in the process. For the Jansenist, man is but an instrument in God's hand. His will is hopelessly corrupt and incapable of choice (except in matters of indifference). For the Thomist, Grace unites with the human will—penetrates it, becomes one with it, raises it above itself, so that, as St Bernard says, the action done is wholly God's and wholly man's[154].

Analogies are dangerous toys, but there is, I think, some truth in saying that the Jansenist position is as if a child were set to draw from a model. He cannot do it—the teacher takes the pencil from him, executes the work, and gives it back to him. The child can only be grateful for what has been done in his stead. According to the Thomist view, the teacher lays his hand upon the child's and guides it; not necessarily making every stroke, but so controlling it that the copy is the work of both together. The child could not do it by himself, cannot make the first mark; but the strong hand has helped him do it and the result is not entirely other than his own.

These are great differences no doubt, but nothing so insuperable as the difference between the heteronymity of the Jansenists and the absolute autonomy of the Molinist, for whom the divine action is juxtaposed to the human will so that the supernatural remains external to the natural, the two working side by side—the teacher helping with advice and encouragement, but the pupil making his own strokes and able to say when all is done, it is a poor thing but my own.

Between Jansenist and Molinist then no terms were possible. But between Jansenist and Thomist a compromise was imaginable, and Arnauld and Nicole set themselves to imagine it.

Arnauld concentrated his attention on sufficient Grace; but he only succeeded in producing a shadowy likeness, and he would not allow it to be universal. Nicole had something more tangible to offer. He thought out a system of general Grace bestowed on all men, giving them the physical capacity of observing God's commandments. This did not, he claimed, invalidate the doctrine of efficacious Grace, which was still necessary in order to remove the voluntary incapacity (as distinguished from the physical capacity) under which all alike labour until they are touched by efficacious Grace. But it has notable effects. By its agency the heathen themselves can nurse degrees and movements of love, which enlighten the mind and warm the will, and which, although not of a nature to win justification, are still directed towards God and enable the accomplishment of acts which are exempt from sin[155].

The development of Nicole's mind along these lines brought him into inevitable conflict with Arnauld (had not Arnauld been at the pains of writing a tract against the so-called virtues of the heathen[156]?), and Nicole's thesis, as formulated about 1680, was denounced as heresy of a malignant type. But he declared that traces of his views were to be found in works of his written long before; he had indeed formed them as early as 1654 or 1656; he had confided them to M. Pascal and the great man had approved them[157].

We need not suppose that Pascal ever went the whole way with Nicole, or that Nicole in 1654 had reached the point which drew upon him Arnauld's thunders in 1680; but there is no question that in the last two *Provincial Letters*, which were written from material supplied by Nicole, the doctrine of the Thomists is treated in a very different spirit from that displayed in the early Letters. There Pascal had laughed at them and their "proximate power," their "insufficient sufficient Grace." There he had included them in the anti-Jansenist coalition and had called them Molinists. Now he treats them very seriously and quotes their doctors with respect[158]. It is all the difference between a controversial fling and a real attempt to understand the others' position, an earnest desire to be found on their side. It is the difference between a brilliant pamphleteer and a man who is beginning to be a theologian. He strains his eyes to see affinities where Jansen was content to register differences, and in the effort, it must be confessed, he neglects or slurs over some crucial points[159]. He feels that after all there is something to be said for sufficient Grace, that the human will is not the purely passive object for the exercise of the divine that once it seemed to him.

All this may be read between the lines of the final *Provinciales*. There are, besides, several unfinished tracts on Grace, in which he clearly displays his desire to solve the problem started in those letters to Mlle Roannez viz. the relation of the human will towards the divine action[160]. He does not solve it. The effort compels him to have recourse to the very subtleties of scholastic thought and terminology which he once derided. They do not help him. He is not really satisfied with either of the competing theories.

The Jansenists sought the determination which inclines to action in the *delectatio*, i.e. the attractive power which external objects exercise upon the will. Pascal is conscious that this power does not depend entirely on the objects or on us. The Thomists placed determination in the *liberum arbitrium*, i.e. a power of choice independent of all objects, or of anything save itself[161]. Pascal feels that this is nonsense. "The power of determining oneself independently from anything except our own determination" conveyed no meaning to him.

He refers determination to a Power above man, and there he leaves it. He knows that the mystery thus confessed must cause both fear and hope; he finds sanction for his practical surrender of the problem in the last scene of the Lord's life, when He gave to the just a lesson of fear in the abandonment of St Peter, and to sinners a lesson of hope in the conversion of the penitent thief. Men must ever humble themselves beneath the hand of God and say with David, "Lord I am not high-minded[162]." This is precisely the tone of his conversation with his confessor. "Once he had engaged in these disputes, but for the last two years he had prudently withdrawn from them in view of the great difficulty of these difficult questions of Grace and Predestination," upon which the safest and indeed the only comment is St Paul's cry, "O the depth of the riches both of the wisdom and the knowledge of God[163]!"

The *Pensées* supply further evidence of a loosening of the strict Jansenist theory. "Man is capable of love and knowledge." "Men are at once unworthy of God and capable of God; unworthy because of their corruption, capable because of their first nature." "He reveals Himself to those who seek Him." "There are two natures in us, the one good, the other evil." "God will free the good nature that is in man from the evil." Man has to seek God, and he can seek first because he is capable of the light. God helps him, delivers him by His Grace. "It needs Grace," says Pascal, "to make a man into a saint; and he that doubts this, knows neither what saint is nor what man is[164]." But Grace solicits the cooperation of man's will. The will must be accessible to the divine compassion. Man does not receive Grace as a merely passive object; he welcomes it, replies to it. "The world exists for the exercise of God's mercy and judgement, not as though men were set in it as they came from His hands, but rather as His enemies to whom He gives by His Grace light enough to return, if they will seek and follow Him; and to punish them if they refuse to seek or follow Him[165]."

No doubt other passages may be quoted on the other side, but so may words which echo that cry of *O altitudo!* "There is surely insupportable presumption in this kind of argument, though it appears to be founded on seeming humility, which is neither sincere nor reasonable if it does not make us confess that we know not of ourselves what we are and can only learn it of God[166]."

But it was not only the teaching of Nicole nor his own self-scrutiny that led Pascal to surrender the hope of certainty in these deep matters. He had the chance, precious to his scientific bent, of putting theory to a practical test. Just when his eyes were opening to the possibility of a *grâce suffisante* and to the creation by God of a living will in man, a subject of experiment was offered in the soul of a friend.

The sister of his Duc de Roannez, Charlotte, was taken with a great desire to become a Port-Royal nun. She believed that God was calling her. She met with much opposition from her mother. Her brother carried her off to Poitou—we may believe, in order to test the truth of her vocation—and while she was there she wrote out all her heart to Pascal. Pieces of nine letters of reply, which concerned her brother as much as herself[167], have been preserved, and they shew us Pascal following, with the wonder of a chemist in presence of a new element, the struggles of a human soul which Grace has certainly touched but which has still to work out its own salvation. The bands of earthly attachment, which seem at first so slender, prove very difficult to break and in the end recover their hold[168].

Mlle de Roannez came out of Port-Royal and died a Duchess, and yet a penitent for having broken her vows[169]. Pascal did not live to see the last act, but what he saw proved to him that God works by no mechanical process, that Grace does not annul liberty, that the double *delectatio* is not a sufficient account of the ultimate relation of the creature towards the Creator. Once more St Paul's words are the best, "O the depth of the riches both of the wisdom and the knowledge of God! how unsearchable are his judgements, and his ways past finding out!"

In this matter indeed Pascal reached no goal, but how far he has travelled since he first touched topics upon which most of his friends felt so secure! He has often been described as a sceptic and a Pyrrhonist, and indeed his whole life is a fever of enquiry, and if he found peace at the last it was not through the satisfaction of his intellect. But his doubts are never directed against the fundamental doctrines which he and we believe to have been revealed by God and to be requisite and necessary to salvation—one God in three Persons; man's access to the Father through the Son, in the Spirit; man's responsibility and God's victorious love. Pascal's *σκέψις* was exercised in a region where it has fair range—the theology by which the human mind seeks to apprehend the doctrine that has been revealed, and gather strength therefrom to live and grow. And if a note of exclamation or of interrogation is his last word on one of the profoundest problems of theology, it is only because the higher principle, the ultimate law which causes and controls the seeming contraries, escapes the ken of man encompassed by infirmity, and teaches, by its self-concealment, a wholesome lesson of humility. For "God," he says, "chooses rather to sway the will than the intellect.

Perfect clearness would be useful to the intellect but would harm the will[170]."

And this confession of ignorance leads him further in the knowledge of Truth than all his search for Truth along the lines he advocates has brought him, and teaches him that the very search is not without its danger. Truth has always been his aim and his love; but now he sees in it a spring of pride, an occasion for the *libido sciendi* which is the Jansenist equivalent of the *ἐπιθυμία τῶν ὀφθαλμῶν* of St John. "We make," he writes, "an idol of Truth itself. For Truth apart from Love is not God, but only His image and an idol which must not be loved or worshipped...I could love total darkness; but if God places me in a state of half darkness, the lack of light displeases me, because I fail to find in it the benefit of total darkness. That is a fault and a sign that I am making an idol of darkness[171]."

The plain meaning of all this subtle arguing is that Pascal, who loved Truth above all else, is looking beyond Truth to the source of Truth, and perceives that the most ardent pursuit of light, the blindest renunciation of one's will and oneself, are after all only means to an end, an end which is as far beyond our comprehension as are the Wisdom and the Knowledge whereby He orders all things, of whom and through whom all things proceed, and to whom they all return.

IV

Blessed are the pure in heart: for they shall see God.
St Matthew v. 8.

It is plain that, unless my reading of the man is all wrong, Pascal was not, in doctrine at least, and to the last, a thoroughgoing Jansenist. In the deep drama that is ever being enacted between the soul and God, he seems, while confessing ignorance of the process, to allow some play of human will, to see a spark in the human breast, which may be fanned to flame by the operation of the divine spirit; he refuses to regard man as a mere puppet; he safeguards his autonomy and freedom. Yet in history he stands with the Jansenists; he cannot be dissociated from them. Why? Mainly because of the morality which they taught and which he was glad to follow.

That morality was austere; it was dark and sunless—of the autumn rather than of the spring. And indeed Saint-Cyran, who was its chief exponent, definitely disliked the spring and its flowers. We are told that they displeased him "because they pass too quickly, and in most cases die without bearing fruit. He preferred the last days of autumn, although only dry and withered leaves are seen upon the trees[172]." And he had no taste for poetry. One day he warned the little scholars of Port-

Royal that Virgil, whom they were conning, was damned for his verses because he had made them out of vanity and to please the world. "You," he added, "may be saved if you learn them for the purpose of pleasing God and fitting yourselves to serve the Church[173]." He discouraged all expression of the emotions, even when prompted by the contrite heart. "I will have," he wrote to a young nun, "no sorrow shewn by means of the senses. Have a care with your tears. No sad looks, no sighs, no gestures—a silence mental and motionless[174]." This severity was reflected in Jansenist public worship; no flowers on the altar, no music in the choir, no appeal to the senses which, as belonging to this vile body, have nothing to do with spiritual exercises. It passed from the sanctuary into common life; it was indeed a corollary of the doctrine of the Fall which had vitiated all human acts. Not only the indulgence but the use of our natural faculties, intellectual as well as sensible, was banned. Withdrawal from the world, self-isolation from social conditions, were preached and practised as sedulously by the Jansenists as by early Christians living in the midst of heathen surroundings and eagerly looking for the Parousia. Asceticism became not only a discipline but an habitual state—the only state befitting man whose duty it was to be rid as quickly as possible of the burden of the flesh and all the ties of human affections[175].

The result was a personal religion of a strongly individualistic type. The Jansenists felt, as few have felt, the mysterious and blessed relations that exist between man and his Maker; but the very intensity with which they saw this truth blurred their vision of the unity and universality of the Church, the congregation of faithful men united to honour God according to the principles of order and direction derived from Him. In the communion to which the Jansenists professed attachment, that unity and universality are represented and summed up by Rome. But to Rome the Jansenists paid but a qualified allegiance[176]. They recognized the supreme dignity of the Apostolic See, but in the primitive Church to which they made regular appeal they found no trace of the secular power[177].

They had, further, special and more modern reasons for mistrusting the Roman *Curia*. The popes, one after another, were openly in favour of those who opposed the *Augustinus*, from which the Jansenists fetched their principles; and by doing so, and by their reasons for so doing, they betrayed their fallibility. The Jansenists' devotion to the Bible and to its vulgarisation through vernacular translation, tended to widen the gulf between ultramontane teachers and themselves[178]. Then the awe with which they regarded the priesthood and its functions inclined them to belittle the earthly channels through which the Grace of Orders is transmitted and to lay all the stress upon the unction of the Spirit. Hence the hierarchy was not always treated by them with blind respect[179].

Finally Jansenist morality was in the last resort founded on the fear of God rather than on His love[180]. The desire of the human heart to enter into union with God, the foundation and root of the religious sentiment, was constantly being baulked by the respect with which their doctors surrounded the very means admitted by them in theory to be sovran for effecting it. Arnauld's book, and in many ways a noble book, *On Frequent Communion* was written at Saint-Cyran's suggestion to guard the altar from profane approach[181]. Truth to tell, he threatens sometimes to render it inaccessible. In his preface he praises pious souls who would be content to defer their communion till their dying hour; in the text he advises a long interval between confession and absolution. The Eucharist tends to become a reward for right-doing rather than a divine help thereto, a medicine rather than a food[182].

Now all these points of Jansenist morality—the deliberate suppression of the aesthetic sense, of the emotions, the marked individualism, the insistence on the awfulness of Almighty God—are reflected in Pascal. But they are sensibly qualified. He has no feeling for poetry; he is contemptuous of art. "How vain a thing is painting, which strives to win admiration by the imitation of things of which we do not admire the originals." He is violently opposed to the stage. "Of all the diversions which the world has invented there is none more dangerous than the play." Yet he had a great dramatic gift and was himself a real poet—not only in the sense in which every great mathematician or natural philosopher is a poet, truly *ἔνθεος*, seeing first in inspired vision the harmonies and relations which after-reflexion enables him to verify[183], but as an artist in words, who knows their value and affective force. All the art of rhetoric is summed up in his account of eloquence, "We must put ourselves into the place of our hearers, and try upon our own heart the turn we give to our discourse, to see whether they are made the one for the other, and whether we can be sure that our hearers will be as it were forced to yield. So far as is possible we must keep to what is natural and simple, not make great what is little, nor little what is great. It is not enough that a phrase be fine, it must suit the subject and not have either excess or defect[184]." And following his instinct, he is the greatest and the first master of French prose, the most delicate instrument for expressing thought that the world has had since Greek.

He kept down the emotions with a ruthless hand. He could not bear to see his sister's children kiss their mother; he would not let her speak of a woman as pretty; he shocked her by the outward coldness with which he received her kindly offices. But we, like her, may well be moved by the inner reason of this restraint. The day he died she learnt from a friend how Blaise had bidden him beware of letting anyone love him with too much attachment: "It was," he said, "a fault which people were not sufficiently careful over, not seeing how serious it was nor considering that by fostering and allowing such attachments they let others take possession of a heart that belonged to God alone and stole from Him what He counted the most precious thing of all[185]."

How hard the sacrifice of feeling was to him is proved by a piece of paper on which he had scribbled *pro memoria*, "It is not fair that any one should attach himself to me, though he do it willingly and gladly. I should be deceiving those in whom I kindled love, for I am no one's final end, and I cannot satisfy them. Am I not doomed to die? Thus the object of their love will die. Therefore as I should be very wrong to give currency to a falsehood, though I should insinuate it gently, though it should be believed with pleasure and caused me pleasure too; in like manner it is very wrong of me if I make myself beloved and draw others to attach themselves to me. I must warn those who are ready to accept a lie not to believe it, whatever profit accrues to me from it; and similarly not to attach themselves to me; for they ought to spend their life and their pains in pleasing God or seeking Him[186]."

That in writing thus and acting thus he did violence to himself is plain from many pleasant fireside sketches that we have of him; he must have been unusually irritable when he chid his sister for her little ones' caresses. He was a real father to his nephew Étienne, taking him to live with him when the Port-Royal school was closed and the boy went to college. Then there was his name-child, Blaise, who, dying in 1684 at the age of thirty, asked to be laid beside him; there were Louis, who was also educated by him, Jacqueline, and the little heroine of the miracle of the Holy Thorn, Marguerite, who has left us interesting memoirs on her family and some not altogether trustworthy anecdotes about her uncle[187].

The children witnessed those last six weeks of Christian endurance, for he spent them under their mother's roof. The reason of his presence there is a monument of his charity. He was housing a family of poor folk just to keep him company. The son caught small-pox. Pascal, who was in desperate need of all his sister's nursing, would not let her come to him because of her children; he would not turn the sick lad out of doors; so he went himself, saying, "To change house is less dangerous for me than for him; so it must be I that move."

His profession of love for the poor for Jesus' sake, which I quoted in my first lecture, was no idle vaunt. Constant sickness was a great drain upon his purse, but he always had money for an alms, even though he had to borrow it from the bankers. When he was reproved for this improvidence he said sharply, "I have noticed one thing, which is that, however poor a man is, he always leaves something at his death." "He had such a love for poverty" (I quote from his sister) "that he kept it always in his thoughts, so that when he went about any undertaking or if anyone wanted his advice, the first thing that came into his head was to consider if anything in this particular case could be done in the service of the poor.... He held that their relief was the universal vocation of all Christians...that to frequent them is extremely profitable, since continual acquaintance with the miseries that oppress them and with their want of bare necessities, even when their diseases are in the most dangerous and deplorable state, is enough to make the hardest heart forgo all useless conveniences and superfluous embellishments[188]."

He reduced his establishment accordingly to its lowest terms and was rebuked by his sister for untidiness[189]. His example and his exhortations fired his friends to suggest methods of organized relief; but he did not approve of this, saying that they were not called upon to deal with the general but with the particular: that he thought the way most pleasing to God was to serve the poor poorly, that is according to each man's ability, without filling the mind with ambitious designs savouring of that seeking after superiority which he ever blamed. Not that he was against the institution of general hospitals; on the contrary he greatly applauded it, as he shewed by his will; but he used to say that these great enterprises were reserved for certain persons whom God destined for the purpose and guided almost visibly. All are not called to that—but all are called to labour daily and individually for the poor[190]. Such views and methods may not command the blessing of the Charity Organisation Society, but at least they testify to an ardent philanthropy. They may not be social, but they are not selfish.

His asceticism, which has been a source of surprise to some and of amusement to others—the menial offices he rendered to himself, making his own bed, carrying his own meals, his enjoyment of his medicines, above all the iron girdle with sharp points which he donned sometimes and drove into his side with his elbow to recall him to his duty when some vain thought or mundane pleasure tempted him[191]—all this was not mere mortification of the flesh, but a real attempt to humble and purify his heart and will; to express by sacrifice and suffering his gratitude to the Lord who had sacrificed Himself and suffered for him, to remind himself violently that he was a man and a man full of sinful impulses. If it is folly, it is the folly of the Cross.

No man's religion was more intensely individual, more profoundly personal; no one ever laid more stress upon the blessedness of direct intercourse with God, nor was more impatient of anything that blocked the immediate vision, nor breathed with greater difficulty the air of passive obedience to authority. The story of the battle round the Formulary tells us that. But he was, equally, against the exaltation of the Ego. "*Le moi est haïssable*: it makes itself the centre of every thing; I shall always hate it." "Everyone is all in all to himself, for when he dies all is dead to him. Hence it comes that he is all things to all men[192]." So his irony turns St Paul's phrase;

unregenerate man regards himself as the sole end of all other beings. Against the enormity of this disproportion Pascal sets the perfectly balanced organism of the Church, wherein each little I has its proper place and function. It is the Body of Christ "by joints and bands having nourishment ministered" from its divine Head. "I am present with thee," says Jesus to him, "by My word in the Scripture, by My Spirit in the Church and by inspiration, by My power in the priest, by My prayer in the faithful[193]." The salvation which has been granted him by God's grace is his, a precious personal gift, but not in isolation, not apart from others. The Church is God's chosen instrument, visibly protected from corruption; the true pastors of the Church, who are the true depositaries of the divine word, have preserved her against the efforts of those who have striven to ruin her. Her history may be strictly called the history of Truth[194].

Pascal and his friends were working in the spirit which has always animated the Church (despite her failures and changes of conduct) to recover and maintain her primitive purity against the relaxed morality which was creeping in. He was in a cleft stick. He saw, to his dismay, the head of that hierarchy with which was bound up the very existence of the Church, lying at the mercy of the promoters of relaxed morality. "It is very easy to take the Pope unawares because of his occupations and the trust he has in the Jesuits; and the Jesuits are very capable of taking him unawares by calumny[195]." Yet, being strongly convinced of the need of unity, he could not shut his eyes to its visible embodiment. Hence there is wild wavering of the needle before it settles down, as it indubitably does, to point steadily Romewards.

To Beurrier he said that he recognized the importance of the Pope's authority and the difficulty of establishing its limits, that, conscious of his own insufficiency in theology, he had decided to withdraw from disputes and controversies which were full of pitfalls for the unwary, and to accept the teaching of the Church on those deep questions of Grace and Predestination, desiring to be in complete submission to the sovran Pontiff who is the Vicar of Jesus Christ[196].

But the head which now at the last was bent so meekly had been proudly raised against Rome two years before. "If my letters are condemned at Rome, what I condemn there is condemned in heaven. *Ad tuum, Domine Jesu, tribunal appello*[197]."

The whole page of MS which contains this solemn appeal to a higher order and authority than Rome, containing, as it does, other thoughts of similar colour, and evidently expressing a deep and passionate conviction, must be set in the scales against utterances making for submission, which can be gathered here and there in his writings[198]. It testifies to a tremendous battle in his breast, and his yielding is another sign of his selflessness and charity. What finally compels obedience is his willingness to sink personal conviction in favour of the general advantage. For close upon the surrender comes a renewed statement of his horror at the relaxed morality which he regarded as the real enemy[199]. There is here no sacrifice of intellectual integrity, but a notable sacrifice of self. It is not the first time nor the last that an honest man has clung to Rome for the sake of the centralized force she can dispose in the conflict against sin and in the task of turning Godwards the souls of men.

The last and in some ways the most striking characteristic of Jansenist morality is its inculcation of a fear of God and of holy things, carried to the length of a strict fencing of the Tables. How does Pascal stand towards this? He has assuredly a fear of God—but he distinguishes between the true fear that comes of faith and the false fear that comes of doubt. True fear is allied to hope, because it is born of faith and because men hope in the God in whom they believe; false fear is allied to despair because they fear the God in whom they do not believe. "The one class fears to lose Him, the other fears to find Him[200]." It is clear, I think, that most of the uneasy cries that break out now and again in the *Pensées* are meant to express the feelings of the second class, as typified by the man whose doubts he is seeking to allay. The true fear sounds in the Mystery of Jesus, but there it is mixed with hope and confidence, as it is indeed whenever a Christian takes up his heritage of freedom, sure of the fact but rejoicing in it with trembling. A *Pensée* helps to illustrate this: "A person said to me one day that when he came from confession he felt great joy and confidence. Another told me that he was still fearful; whereupon I thought that these two together would make one good man and that each was wanting in that he lacks the feeling of the other[201]."

The fear and the trembling were constantly in play with Jansenist teachers. A frown is on their brow, the word 'terrible' is ever on their lips. God is terrible, the Virgin is terrible, the priesthood is a terrible mystery, preaching is as terrible a mystery as the Eucharist—nay Saint-Cyran thought it even more terrible[202]. But what Pascal requires is not terror but religion. "The conduct of God, who disposes all things gently, is to put religion into the mind by reason and into the heart by Grace. But to try to put it into the mind and heart by force and menace, is not to put religion there but terror—*terrorem potius quam religionem*." Such words have not the true Jansenist ring[203].

At the same time passages are not wanting which shew adherence to the principles announced in the book on Frequent Communion[204]. And Pascal had the most profound veneration for the Eucharist, in whose Species he found the hidden manna and beheld the secret dwelling of the God that hideth Himself[205]. But would he ever have subscribed to Arnauld's praise of deferred communion? Come to his death-bed and judge! The Jansenist dread of unworthy participation was never plainly or more painfully displayed than by those who stood round him then. He knew he was dying and he earnestly and repeatedly asked for the Sacrament. The doctors pooh-poohed his apprehensions. "There is no shadow of danger," they said. His friends supported the doctors—told him he was much better and could well wait until he could go to church in proper form. He was much troubled, but he gave way. A fancy, an infinitely touching fancy took him. "Since they will not let me communicate in the Head, let me communicate in the members. Give me a poor man to live with me and have like service done to him as to myself....Ask M. le Curé to send me a sick man for the purpose." No sick man was available, but he was promised an old man to look after as soon as he was cured. Pascal knew that would never be, and begged as an immediate alternative that he might be carried to the common hospital to die among the poor. So the time wore on with frequent confessions and gentle protestations on Pascal's part, but no complaint; until at last his state alarmed his sister and at his request she had the parish priest, our friend M. Beurrier, no Jansenist, fetched to him. He entered the room, bearing the Elements, and cried, "Here is the Holy One whom you have so much longed for." The words roused Pascal. He answered the questions of the priest distinctly, "Yes, sir, all that I believe with all my heart." He received the Viaticum and Extreme Unction with tears of love and joy. And when he was blessed with the ciborium he cried, "May God never leave me," and died[206]. One only comment is possible on this scene: "through ignorance they did it."

What then has this man to teach us, with his variations, his controversies, his extravagances? First and foremost, he teaches us to face the facts: to have done with canting, as Dr Johnson said. He looks out upon the world and in upon himself and tries to see men and things as they really are. His eye, whichever way he turns it, lights upon seeming contradictions; but he will not let himself be wearied or bewildered. He continues his steady gaze; he tries a new angle, another point of view, and with the change of perspective what seemed a conglomeration breaks up into a series of points. He grasps with both hands the two ends of the chain, although the intervening links remain hidden from sight. He holds the contraries in balance[207] and searches patiently for the superior principle that shall explain and unify them. In a word, he shews himself the true man of science, who will not pronounce judgement till he has tried every hypothesis, and if no satisfactory hypothesis presents itself, he will wait till it does.

A glance convinces him that nothing in the world is stable. *Πάντα ῥεῖ.* Life is on the move between two infinities—the infinitely great and the infinitely little. However large a number is, however vast a space, however long a time, one must always be prepared to find a further number, a larger space, a longer time, and *vice versa.* In other words his infinity is mathematical rather than metaphysical[208]. But although everything is unstable, although we can see neither beginning nor end, nothing is in confusion. Things move, but they move in order, and all things in their several orders. By orders he means groups of similars, the natural classes into which all objects of sight and thought may be arranged. There is an order of the heart, of the mind, of the flesh. "All nature's truths are self-contained. Our *art* encloses them one within another, but that is not according to nature. Each holds its own place[209]."

This theory of orders runs through all his thought, starting from his letter to the Queen of Sweden that went with the calculating machine[210]. It is convincingly handled in the instructions to the young nobleman which I have already mentioned[211]; it appears repeatedly in the *Pensées,* most triumphantly of all in one which is meant to refute the objections raised against Christ's divinity from a consideration of His lowly state. Pascal shews that this state is proper to Jesus Christ because He belongs to the Spiritual Order. "Kings and captains in their carnal order have their proper greatness which all are bound to admit. Wise men have theirs and we pay them the homage of the mind. The Saints have theirs, they have their empire, their glory, their victory, their lustre, and want no glory of the flesh or of the mind, with which they have nothing to do, for these add nothing to them, nor take aught away. Jesus is the most signal example of this Order. He has no peer. How ridiculous then to be shocked at the lowness of His condition, which is of quite another order. All bodies—the firmament, the stars, the earth and its kingdoms—are not comparable to mind at its lowest. All bodies together and all minds together are not worth the least motion of charity. This is of an order infinitely more exalted. From all bodies together we cannot extract one little thought; from all bodies and all minds it is impossible to produce a single motion of true charity; it is impossible, it belongs to another and a supernatural order. To the rich their riches, to the great their rank, to the wise their wisdom, and to Jesus His Holiness. It would have been needless to our Lord Jesus Christ for the purpose of shining in His kingdom of holiness to come as kings come; but He did come in the glory proper to His order. He gave no great invention to the world, He never reigned; but He was humble, meek, holy, holy before God, terrible to devils, without spot of sin. O in what great pomp and in what marvellous splendour did He come to the eyes of the heart[212]!"

Here are lessons which we should do well to ponder. Not only in the high regions to which these words of Pascal lift us, but in our every day dealings we are constantly confusing the orders. Our failure to distinguish them is responsible for half the wrong imputation of motives, and for more than half the envy and the disappointed personal ambitions with which we vex ourselves and others. And does not a special point which vexes so many souls to-day arise partly from a failure to distinguish orders? Big battalions and Dreadnoughts and "reeking shards" belong to a certain order, the order of the sword not borne in vain, a carnal order, an order waxing old, we trust, and ready to vanish away, which yet here and now commands our respect and compels our use for the punishment of vice and the vindication of virtue. We may surely use them concurrently with a weapon of another and a higher order, the appeal by prayer to Him whose cause we are fain to think our own, but whose Will whatever its issues we accept—provided always that we keep the two orders apart and do not superstitiously or vaingloriously look to either for effects which do not properly belong to it.

Pascal presents in a singularly striking form a singularly persuasive apologetic. The witness of the soul's experience to God; the hunger for the Light as evidence for the existence of the Light; the claim that the heart is already in possession of what it seeks, not by discursive reasoning but by immediate apprehension. "The heart sensible to God." "Thou wouldst not be seeking me, hadst thou not already found me[213]." This is Pascal's argument which most moves modern men. By heart he means love, faith, will, instinct, feeling, nature—the intuition which plays its part in every province of human activity. He does not ask us to use in religion a faculty which is unfamiliar to us elsewhere. Intuition is at work in every kind of speculation[214]. What man of science will deny the truth of this? Discursive reasoning has its place, but a secondary place. It is of another order.

There were phrases and notions born of mystical contemplation current in Pascal's day which might possibly have floated into his study. Santa Teresa had conquered a certain section of French devout society. Her Biography was known by those who mistrusted her tendencies as the Bible of the Bigots[215]. And she had spoken of "visions with the eyes of the soul"; she had "simply felt Christ close by her." And Tomaso Campanella, the Calabrian Dominican, whose spiritual vision rack and dungeon could not dim, had in a book published in Paris in 1638 taught, as it had not been taught before, the knowledge of God not by syllogism, not by authority, but by the inward touch—*tactus intrinsecus*[216].

Pascal was a mystic; his Memorial has all the authentic marks, and such language as I have quoted would have found an echo in his heart. There is no doubt that he walked in the enchanted garden; he appears to have been conversant, for instance, with Nicolaus of Cusa[217]. But he mentions Santa Teresa but once, and Campanella never, and it is improbable that they influenced him. And after all there is no need to hunt down connexions and affinities, more or less obscure, in writers whom Pascal may or may not have read. If he sought confirmation of the truth of his intuition, he had St Augustine and St Paul. He would remember "the flash of one trembling glance" with which Augustine's "mind arrived at that which IS," and how he described a state of love before which the temporal things, assumed by Christ for our sake, fall into a secondary place as a means of knowledge[218]. Above all he would remember how St Paul had been won to Jesus Christ not by the history of the earthly life, but by the sight of the glorious and ascended Lord and by the sound of a voice from His lips; he knew that he had himself seen something that November night. And the glory and the certainty with which it filled his heart compelled him to appeal to it as the best evidence for the Love of God, and to point others to their heart as the seat of Light and Grace, if only they would look.

In a word, to borrow terms of modern jargon, he knew at first hand what the Immanence of the Transcendent is, and he is naturally and rightly taken by those who found their apologetic upon Immanence as their leader[219]. What is this apologetic, this method of Immanence? There are other methods—there is the Transcendental method. The Christian story is presented as a series of marvellous events, supported by historical evidence, worthy of credence and leading him who accepts it to the knowledge of the Saviour and to Faith in Him. This method has its fruit in blessed results, for Christ, however preached, brings peace. But according to it, on any shewing, Christianity is outside the man at first, and he takes it into himself. It starts with an appeal to his reason; it supports its conclusions by analogies, sometimes telling, sometimes weak and out of date, when theology lags behind science.

The apologetic founded upon Immanence has a different point of departure. It goes back and down to the desire and the compulsion to learn what we are and whither we are tending; what is our destiny and how we are to fulfil it. Impelled by this need and longing we look out for help, and we find in Christ the satisfaction of our want and the explanation of our being:

> Only the deep desire of my heart cries out
> By all the thunder of its want and woe,
> Cries out to Thee.

Christianity is here not a piece of the supernatural laid upon the natural: it is the supernatural interpenetrating and interpreting the natural. We may of course easily exaggerate the power of this appeal. There is always the danger of self-delusion, of forcing the will to believe —the danger that the figure of the divine Consoler is merely the projection of the believer's mind, his boasted experience but a passing emotion[220]. There is the tendency to surrender the idea of any manifestation of the supernatural outside the natural, to let miracles go by the board, to say good-bye to tradition, revelation, church, and sacraments, to substitute one idolatry for another, the infallible soul for the infallible church or the infallible book.

Pascal at least did not run that risk. Assuredly he did not neglect historical evidence. We know how he valued the Bible, what stress he laid on miracles, how mightily he wielded the argument from prophecy. No, in adopting another new line of apologetic he did not lay aside the old. But like the man of science that he was, he starts from the best known, the heart, and he finds the explanation of man's misery in the Biblical scheme of Redemption. "Without the Scripture which has Jesus Christ alone for its object, we know nothing, and see only obscurity and confusion in God's nature and our own[221]." And he gives due weight to Reason. Nothing is more untrue than to say he pays no heed to it. Every line he wrote, every thought he expressed, bear witness to a wonderful gift of Reason wonderfully applied. The logic of his plan is exceedingly clear and cogent. He says hard things of the intellectual faculty by which judgements are formed; he refuses it the right to judge the heart, he denies the power of philosophy to tell man the truth about himself. But he has reasons for his refusal. He judges Reason by itself and its evident failures. And remember that according to his own statement he does not set out to prove, but to suggest; to open the heart, and prepare the will. Then, but not till then, the faculty of Reason—the Thought which is man's glory—comes into play. To apply it in the first instance is to court rationalism, self-sufficiency, and ruin[222].

Once more, following the spirit if not the letter of his exposition, we may sit at Pascal's feet. We will not put upon the immanental method more weight than it will bear. We will hold fast what is good, while we prove all things; we will admit the appeal to miracles, regarding them not as interferences with the natural breaking in upon it from outside, but as manifestations of a higher order which is all around us, within us and without. We shall read as a sign from God every event that has a spiritual content[223]. And we shall remember that according to St John our blessed Lord found many who believed in His name, seeing His signs which He did and who yet did not trust themselves to Him; that Nicodemus, drawn by His signs, came to Him by night; that many Samaritans believed in Him because of His signs, but more believed because of His own words to them; that finally He put Himself and His union with the Father as the prime means of conviction. "Believe me that I am in the Father, and the Father in me; or else believe me for the very works' sake[224]."

We shall thankfully remark the fulfilment of prophecy, but we shall think more about the general tenor of its witness to Messiah than about the details of its forecast. But we shall recognize that the holiness of miracles and the pearls of prophecy are only discernible by the softened heart, the pure heart, and the will and the reason enlightened by Grace, without which man, as Pascal says, is no better than the brutes[225].

From his life, viewed as a whole, we learn the possibility of combining independence of belief with loyalty to the body of which we are members. I must praise God not only for this heart of mine which discerns and loves Him, but for the share of service which He gives me in spreading His name through channels and by means approved of Him. The unspeakable gift for which St Paul thanks God is not the glories and revelations vouchsafed to him in person, but that "He maketh manifest through us the savour of His knowledge in every place[226]." We need to temper mysticism with the steadying influence of an institutional religion. We cannot yet dispense with law and guidance. The mystic who refuses discipline in reliance on his Inner Light falls easily into dangerous delusions.

Now one of the notes in Pascal's Memorial is "Absolute submission to Jesus Christ and to my director." Obedience was not difficult to him when the voice of Christ and of the Church spoke in harmony. But there came times when loyalty to Truth and to himself seemed to clash with loyalty to the visible head of the Church, and then he cries aloud as if in pain, "I will never sever myself from his communion[227]."

This dilemma is happily not presented to those for whom unity is not symbolized by the bishop of a single see, however venerable, but is contained in a living organism, one in faith, in administration, in worship.

We to whom ultramontanism is a deformation of the truth may regret Pascal's final surrender, but we cannot but admire his self-effacement and his loyalty, and be thankful that we are not called upon to make a like choice, and pray we may be spared the pain of a conflict between the right of private judgement, which we so dearly cherish, and the loyalty which we owe the Church we love.

Authority and private judgement are doubtless contraries, but contraries that we can hold without too great a strain, if we believe we possess the principle that reconciles them.

Lastly, Pascal teaches us holiness of life. No one can lay down the story of his last days without being moved. He lived on heights inaccessible to most. But he did not come down from heaven to stand there; he climbed up painfully out of a dark valley. He shews us the steps as plainly as he shewed them to his generation.

I claimed for him at the outset the saintly qualities of mercy and truth; and if the mercy was not native to him nor won without a struggle, without Grace, it shines the brighter for the dark cloud of irritability and self-will through which it broke. "The extraordinary vivacity of his mind," we read, "made him sometimes so impatient that it was difficult to please him. But when you took notice of it to him, or when he observed that his impatience had vexed anyone, he made immediate amends for it by such a courteous behaviour that he never lost anybody's friendship thereby[228]." His fortitude in bearing the most acute bodily suffering, not lessened by the medicine of his day, amazed his friends. When they pitied him openly he said, "Sickness is the natural state of a Christian....Is it not a great happiness to be by necessity in that state in which we ought to be, and to having nothing else to do but humbly and peaceably to submit to it? For this reason all I ask is to beseech God to grant me this favour[229]." "He is indeed a child; he is humble and submissive as a babe," was the verdict of one who saw him at the end[230]. But this patience and meekness were not easily acquired; the taming of his natural man taxed all his vigilance.

His inclination was to have everything about him of the best, yet no Christian Socialist could be more scrupulous in bestowing his custom. "One should always choose," he said, "the poorest and honestest workmen, and not hunt after that sort of excellence which is never necessary nor can ever be useful[231]." And if the mercy and consideration which he consulted in dealing with his fellows of high or low degree may seem to have failed him now and then in controversy, we must think of the zeal for truth which put the edge on his weapon, and further remember that his greatest and unfinished work was prompted by a movement of charity. In his Apology there is not one grain of personal ambition; there is some irritation with the atheists who strive or sin against the light: "if a doubter is gay and presumptuous, I have no words in which to describe so extravagant a creature,"—but chiefly a great pity for those who doubt and weep to doubt. "Are they not unhappy enough already[232]?" And love for man, despite his vileness, is the dominant note of his *Pensées*—love of man for Jesus' sake.

Surely Pascal was a saint. For after all what is a

Christian saint? One set apart for the service of a holy God, and therefore wearing some reflexion of His holiness—one who bears on his body the marks of the Lord Jesus, and on his visage the evidence of having been with Him; who minds not earthly things, who holds the Head and discerns the Body, who lives in perpetual union with Christ and His members, who loves Truth and follows Mercy.

This man was not altogether Truth nor altogether Mercy; he did not attain to the perfect likeness of the God he served. But perfect likeness is denied to all the sons of men save One. We cannot hope to win more than half-likeness, though our destiny is to pass through it into whole-likeness. One of our helps toward attaining half-likeness is the example of those who by God's Grace are further on the road than we, and nearer to the mark. Pascal is of these. Whatever be our differences of view on Grace and Free-will, on Predestination, on the doctrine of the Church and Sacraments, on asceticism, on casuistry, on the Fall, on miracles, on the fulfilment of prophecy, we cannot withhold from Pascal the homage due to one who ever loved Truth and taught himself to practise Mercy, or rather, as he himself has phrased it, who was brought to Truth and Mercy by God's infinite Grace, and who saw God because his eye was single and his heart was pure.

At the close of these lectures I feel that some apology is due to those who have heard me patiently, and to the memory of the great man with some aspects of whose character and genius I have tried to deal. And apart from the manner of the treatment, it may fairly be asked whether the subject is a fitting one for Hulsean lectures?

Upon which point I have but this to say. One soul at least has by the hurried preparation for the course been brought to feel in a peculiar degree the Truth and Excellence of Christianity, as exemplified in the person of Blaise Pascal, and has found fresh evidence for Revealed Religion in his teaching[233]; and if the imperfect results of that preparation turn a single hearer towards the original, it will not have been attempted altogether in vain.

NOTES

I quote the *Pensées* by their numbers in Brunschvicg's editions; the spelling has been restored wherever possible by aid of the Facsimile.

I quote the *Provinciales* from the text of the edition in "Les Grands Écrivains de la France."

I quote other works contained in this edition as "Pascal, *Œuvres*," etc.

1 p. 2. Cf. "J'ose prendre le parti de l'humanité contre ce misanthrope sublime." Voltaire, *Lettres Philosophiques*, xxv.

"Son cerveau se dérangea sur les dernières années de sa vie, qui fut courte." *Examen important de milord Bolingbroke* (1767).

To these quotations may be added the following:

"Ne vous lassez pas de dire que depuis l'affaire du Pont de Neuilly, Pascal avait perdu la tête."

These last words or their equivalent are commonly attributed to Voltaire, writing to Condorcet. They do not appear in his published correspondence, but there is no doubt that they represent his opinion.

The *affaire du pont de Neuilly* depends on the following solitary testimony contained in a MS. of the Oratorians at Clermont:

"M. Arnoul, curé de Chamboursy, dit qu'il a appris de M. le Prieur de Barillon, ami de Mme Périer, que M. Pascal, quelques années avant sa mort, étant allé, selon sa coutume, un jour de fête, à la promenade au pont de Neuilly avec quelques-uns de ses amis, dans un carrosse à quatre ou six chevaux, les deux chevaux de volée prirent le mors aux dents à l'endroit du pont où il n'y avoit point de garde-fou; et s'étant précipités dans l'eau, les laisses qui les attachoient au train de derrière se rompirent, en sorte que le carrosse demeura sur le bord du précipice. Ce qui fit prendre la résolution à M. Pascal de rompre ses promenades et de vivre dans une entière solitude."

That there was an accident we may believe; that it had all the consequences which the good fathers and, of course, Condorcet and Voltaire, attributed to it we may doubt. Pascal nowhere mentions it. The most interesting fact connected with the story is the evidence of the style in which Pascal was living in 1654, and the best examination of the evidence for it is contained in V. Giraud's *Blaise Pascal* (1910), pp. 36–63, "Une légende de la vie de Pascal."

2 p. 3. "J'ayme la pauvreté parce qu'il la aymée. J'ayme les biens parce qu'ils donnent le moyen d'en assister les miserables. Je garde fidelité à tout le monde, je ne rends pas le mal à ceux qui m'en font; mais je leur souhaitte une condition pareille à la mienne, où l'on ne reçoit pas de mal ni de bien de la part des hommes. J'essaye d'estre juste, véritable, sincere et fidele à tous les hommes; et j'ay une tendresse de cœur pour ceux à qui Dieu m'a uni plus estroictement; et soit que je sois seul, ou à la veue des hommes, j'ay en toutes mes actions la veue de Dieu qui les doit juger, et à qui je les ay toutes consacrées. Voilà quels sont mes sentiments, et je bénis tous les jours de ma vie mon Redempteur qui les a mis en moy et qui, d'un homme plein de foiblesses, de miseres, de concupiscence, d'orgueil et d'ambition, a fait un homme exempt de tous ces maux par la force de sa grace, à laquelle toute la gloire en est deue, n'ayant de moy que la misere et l'erreur." *Pensées*, no. 550.

This *Pensée* is also quoted with slight variations by Mme Perier in her *Vie de M. Pascal* prefixed to the "Port-Royal" and most subsequent editions of the *Pensées.*

3 p. 3. On the Pascal family, see Sainte-Beuve, *Port-Royal,* t. ii, pp. 454 ff.

4 p. 4. He was President of the *Cour des Aides,* a court which heard and determined all causes relating to the levy of *aides* or indirect taxes.

5 p. 4. His wife, *née* Antoinette Begon, died in 1626.

6 p. 4. (i) Gilberte, † 1687, married Florin Perier, *Conseiller* at the *Cour des Aides,* Clermont; (ii) Blaise, 1623–1662; (iii) Jacqueline (La Sœur Jacqueline de Sainte-Euphémie), † 1661.

7 p. 4. Cf. Mme Perier's *Vie de M. Pascal.*

8 p. 4. Cf. Victor Cousin, *Jacqueline Pascal* (1849), pp. 27 ff., 58 ff.

9 p. 4. Étienne Pascal's savings were invested in bonds upon the *Hôtel de Ville.* These bonds being reduced in value by the government, the annuitants expostulated with vigour of word and action. There was in fact something like an *émeute* which Richelieu dealt with summarily. Pascal *père* only escaped the Bastille by burying himself in Auvergne.

10 p. 4. Rouville in the canton of Bolbec near Le Havre. The *curé's* name was Guillebert; he was a friend of Saint-Cyran's, who addressed to him the "Lettres sur le sacerdoce." Cf. *Lettres chrétiennes et spirituelles* (ed. 1744), t. i. His followers were called *Rouvillistes.*

Cf. "On venoit l'entendre prêcher de tous les environs; et il y avoit même des Officiers du Parlement de Rouen, qui louoient des appartemens à Rouville, pour y venir coucher les samedis." *Recueil de plusieurs pièces pour servir à l'Histoire de Port-Royal* ("*Recueil d'Utrecht*") (1740), p. 249.

11 p. 5. "Le frère et la sœur porterent ensuite Monsieur leur père à se donner pleinement à Dieu." *Recueil d'Utrecht*, p. 252.

12 p. 5. Cf. F.-V. Bouquet, *Points obscurs de la vie de Pierre Corneille* (1888), pp. 31 ff.

13 p. 5. Cf. Strowski, *Pascal et son temps*, t. i, ch. 2, "Le courant stoïcien" and t. ii, p. 47. Most of the editions of the works of Du Vair were printed at Rouen.

14 p. 5. Cf. Cousin, *Jacqueline Pascal*, pp. 63–66.

15 p. 5. Cf. Strowski, *op. cit.* t. ii, p. 53.

16 p. 6. Cf. Strowski, *op. cit.* t. ii, pp. 69 ff., 79.

17 p. 6. Cf. Cousin, *op. cit.* p. 60.

18 p. 7. This would explain the interest which the other sister, Mme Perier, took and the part which she played in the matter. One thing is clear. There was no injustice done or intended. A nun could not inherit. On the whole question cf. Ch.-H. Boudhours, reviewing Strowski, in *L'Enseignement secondaire* for December, 1907.

19 p. 7. "Or vous saviez bien que celui qui a le plus d'intérêt à cette affaire est encore trop du monde, et mesme dans la vanité et les amusemens, pour preferer les aumosnes que vous vouliez faire à sa commodité particulière; et de croire qu'il auroit assez d'amitié pour le faire à votre consideration, c'étoit esperer une chose inouie et impossible. Cela ne se pouvoit faire sans miracle; je dis un miracle de nature et d'affection; car il n'y avoit pas lieu d'attendre un miracle de grace en une personne comme luy; et vous savez bien qu'il ne faut jamais s'attendre aux miracles." Jacqueline to the Prioress of Port-Royal, 10 June 1653, *ap.* V. Cousin, *op. cit.* pp. 133–177. For a better text see Pascal, *Œuvres*, t. iii. pp. 51–94.

20 p. 8. There is an excellent account of Rambouillet and *honnêteté* in A. Tilley's *From Montaigne to Molière* (1908), ch. v.

21 p. 8. La Rochefoucauld's *Maximes* appeared between 1659 and 1664.

22 p. 9. "J'aime Paris et la Cour, le jeu, la Musique, les Balets, l'entretien d'un honneste homme et d'une femme agréable et tant d'autres divertissemens qu'on trouve en ce grand Monde. Mais je ne croy pas tout perdre en les perdant. Il me vient d'autres plaisirs qui me consolent de ceux que je n'ay plus. J'ayme les chants des oiseaux dans les bocages, le murmure d'une eau vive et claire, et les cris des troupeaux dans une Prairie. Tout cela me fait sentir une douceur naturelle et tranquille qu'on ne connoît point dans le tumulte et dans

l'embarras de Paris." Méré to Mitton, *Œuvres de M. de Méré* (ed. 1692), t. ii, p. 108.

23 p. 9. He is quoted once in the *Pensées* in a passage which throws light on his character and on the genesis of Pascal's own reflexions:

"M. de Roannez disoit: 'Les raisons me viennent apres, mais d'abord la chose m'agrée ou me choque sans en savoir la raison, et cependant cela me choque par cette raison que je ne decouvre qu'ensuite.' Mais je crois, non pas que cela choquoit par ces raisons qu'on trouve apres, mais qu'on ne trouve ces raisons que parce que cela choque." *Pensées*, no. 276.

24 p. 9. She had helped to interest her uncle, Richelieu, in the Pascals and had commended Blaise to him as "fort savant en mathématiques et qui n'a pourtant que quinze ans." See above, p. 6.

25 p. 10. Cf. Sainte-Beuve, *op. cit.* t. v, pp. 51 ff.

26 p. 10. "*Divertissement*...De là vient que le jeu et la conversation des femmes, la guerre, les grands employs sont si recherchés. Ce n'est pas qu'il y ayt en effect de bonheur, ni qu'on s'imagine que la vraye beatitude soit d'avoir l'argent qu'on peut gagner au jeu, ou dans le lievre qu'on court: on n'en voudroit pas s'il estoit offert...c'est le tracas qui nous détourne d'y penser et nous divertit...Ainsi (l'homme) est si vain, qu'estant plein de nulles causes essentielles d'ennuy, la moindre chose, comme un billard et une balle qu'il pousse, suffisent pour le divertir." *Pensées*, no. 139.

"On vient de lui servir une balle, et il faut qu'il la rejette à son compagnon, il est occupé à la prendre à la cheute du toit, pour gacgner une chasse;...Voilà un soing digne d'occuper cette grande ame et de luy oster toute autre pensée de l'esprit." *Pensées*, no. 140.

27 p. 10. Cf. Strowski, *op. cit.* t. ii, pp. 230–234.

28 p. 11. Letters to Mme Perier, 8 December 1654 and 25 January 1655, printed by V. Cousin in *Jacqueline Pascal*, pp. 188–195. Cf. Pascal, *Œuvres*, t. iv, pp. 2 ff., 61 ff.

29 p. 11. "Deux ans devant sa mort il fist de grandes aumosnes et vendit son carrosse, ses chevaux, ses tapisseries, ses beaux meubles, son argenterie, et même sa bibliothèque, à la réserve de la Bible, de Saint Augustin, et de fort peu d'autres livres, et en donna tout l'argent aux pauvres."

Statement by Père Beurrier, printed for the first time by E. Jovy in *Pascal Inédit*, t. ii (1910), p. 494.

30 p. 11. See Strowski, *op. cit.* t. ii. Appendix on *Les réunions savantes au milieu du dix-septième siècle.*

31 p. 11. Cf. Todhunter, *History of Mathematical theory of Probability* (1865), ch. II.

32 p. 12. Cf. the chapter, "Pascal a-t-il été amoureux?" in V. Giraud's *Blaise Pascal* (1910), pp. 142–197.

33 p. 12. *Prière pour demander à Dieu le bon usage des maladies* assigned by tradition and by M. Brunschvicg (*Pensées et Opuscules*, p. 56) to the time of the first conversion, but by M. Strowski with, I think, greater probability to the time of the second conversion. Cf. Strowski, *op. cit.* ii, pp. 353 ff.

34 p. 12. Does the *Feu* which stands at the head of the Memorial refer to the divine fire which is a regular feature of mystical rapture (cf. Fr. von Hügel, *The Mystical Element in Religion* (1908), vol. i, pp. 178 ff.; E. Underhill, *The Mystic Way* (1913), pp. 323 ff.); or is it simply an allusion to *Ps.* xxxix. 3 *Et in meditatione mea exardescet ignis*?

35 p. 12. Cf. "Il me semble que vous aviez mérité...d'être encore quelque temps importuné de la senteur du bourbier que vous aviez embrassé avec tant d'empressement." Jacqueline to Blaise, 19 January 1655: *ap.* V. Cousin, *op. cit.* pp. 195 ff. Cf. Pascal, *Œuvres*, t. ii, pp. 17 ff.

36 p. 13. Cf. "La mathématique...est inutile en sa profondeur." *Pensées*, no. 61.

"Je la trouve (la géometrie) le plus haut exercice de l'esprit, mais en mesme temps je la connois pour si inutile que je fais peu de différence entre un homme qui n'est que geomètre et un habile artisan." Pascal to Fermat. See below, note 38.

37 p. 13. Cf. "Quoiqu'il soit très difficile d'aborder M. Pascal, et qu'il soit tout à fait retiré pour se donner entièrement à la dévotion, il n'a pas perdre de vue les mathématiques. Lorsque M. de Carcavy le peut recontrer, et qu'il lui propose quelque question, il ne lui en refuse pas la solution, et principalement sur le sujet des jeux de hasard, qu'il a le premier mis sur le tapis." Mylon to Huygens, 2 March 1657, *ap.* Strowski, *op. cit.* t. iii, p. 326.

38 p. 13. Cf. "Vous êtes le plus galant homme du monde, et je suis assurément un de ceux qui sçay le mieux reconnoistre ces qualitéz-là et les admirer infiniment, surtout quand elles sont jointes aux talens qui se trouvent singulierement en vous...Je vous diray aussi que, quoy que vous soyez celuy de toute l'Europe que je tiens pour le plus grand Geometre, ce ne seroit pas cette qualité-là qui m'auroit attiré; mais que je me figure tant d'esprit et d'honnêteté en votre conversation, que c'est pour cela que je vous rechercherois." Pascal to Fermat, 10 August 1660, *Œuvres*, t. x, p. 4.

39 p. 14. *Trois discours sur la condition des grands. Pensées et Opuscules*, pp. 231–238, *Œuvres*, t. ix, pp. 365–373. The boy was probably the eldest son of the Duc de Luynes and was afterwards Duc de Chevreux, the friend of Fénelon and Saint-Simon. He was fourteen or fifteen years old when these *Discours* were written in 1660.

40 p. 14. "Ce que je vous dis ne va pas bien loin; et si vous en demeurez là, vous ne laisserez pas de vous perdre; mais au moins vous vous perdrez en honneste homme." *Pensées et Opuscules*, p. 238, *Œuvres*, t. ix, p. 372.

41 p. 15. Cf. Jovy, *op. cit.* t. ii, p. 494 note.

42 p. 15. Cf. *Vie de M. Pascal.*

43 p. 15. Cf. "Vous ne manquerez pas neantmoins de dire que je suis de Port-Royal....Je sçay, mes Peres, le merite de ces pieux solitaires... je sçay combien ils ont de pieté et de lumiere. Car encore que je n'aye jamais eu d'establissement avec eux...je ne laisse pas d'en connoistre quelques-uns et d'honnorer la vertu de tous." xvie *Provinciale.*

"Je n'ay qu'à vous dire que je n'en suis pas, et à vous renvoyer à mes Lettres, où j'ay dit 'que je suis seul,' et, en propres termes, que 'je ne suis point de Port-Royal,' comme j'ay fait dans la 16." xviie *Provinciale.*

44 p. 15. See Sainte-Beuve, *op. cit.* t. i, l. 1, "Origines et Renaissance de Port-Royal."

45 p. 16. See Sainte-Beuve, *op. cit.* t. iii, iv; F. Cadet, *L'Education à Port-Royal* (1887).

46 p. 16. After describing the effect of the miracle on the general public ("tout Paris"), on the child's father, M. Perier, and on her uncle, M. Pascal, Fontaine starts a fresh paragraph as follows:

"Mais ce que j'admirai alors, fut la manière dont ces Messieurs, et principalement M. de Saci, parloient du miracle," etc. *Mémoires pour servir à l'Histoire de Port-Royal*, t. iii, p. 190 (ed. of 1753).

The miracle was wrought at Port-Royal de Paris, now a Maternity Hospital in the rue Port-Royal.

47 p. 17. Luynes and his pious Duchess built themselves a little château (Vaumurier) within a hundred yards of the convent of Port-Royal des Champs. When she died, the Duke took the Solitaries to live with him in the still uncompleted building and was very active in the work of enlarging and improving the convent for the nuns. See Sainte-Beuve, *op. cit.* t. ii, p. 314 ff.

48 p. 17. On January 7, 1655, two years and a half after Pascal's death, Hardouin de Péréfixe, Archbishop of Paris, sent for M. Beurrier, *curé* of Saint-Étienne-du-Mont, and asked him whether it was true that M. Pascal had died in his parish and without receiving the Sacraments. Beurrier replied that he had himself confessed him and administered the Sacraments to him. "How could you do that, knowing him to be a Jansenist?" Beurrier answered that Pascal had always appeared to him orthodox and obedient to the Church and the Pope, and that in private conversation he had admitted a previous connexion with the Party from which however he had withdrawn for two years past, because he noticed that

ces messieurs went too far (*allaient trop avant*) in the matters of Grace and seemed to be less submissive than they ought to be to the Pope. The Archbishop there and then committed this statement to writing, made Beurrier sign it, and published it, much against his wishes. The Jesuits naturally made the most of this "retraction"; the Jansenists, no less naturally, sought to minimize it and in fact succeeded after long and repeated efforts in extracting from Beurrier an admission, in 1671, that after all he might have misunderstood the sick man.

"J'ai bien reconnu que ces paroles pouvoient avoir un autre sens que celui que je leur avois donné." Beurrier to Mme Perier, 12 June 1671.

He even tacitly accepts the suggestion that Pascal, so far from meaning that *ces messieurs* went too far in matters of Grace, really meant that they did not go far enough, and did not shew that loyalty to Jansenist principles which he expected and of which he had himself given them an example.

The matter was still being canvassed in 1701, i.e. forty years after Pascal's death and seven years after Beurrier's. Since then it has generally been believed that Beurrier's palinode settled the question. See Sainte-Beuve, *op. cit.* t. iii. But in 1908 M. Ernest Jovy discovered in the Memoirs of Beurrier an independent account by him of what happened at Pascal's death-bed. This document, which is printed at length in *Pascal Inédit*, t. iii, pp. 487 ff., supports in all essential details the declaration which Beurrier made before the Archbishop. It is so important that I venture to quote the salient passages.

"Je n'ay point connu monsieur Paschal que six semaines avant sa mort lorsqu'il...m'envoia quérir pour me consulter sur les affaires de sa conscience, et, après le salut mutuel, il me dit qu'ayant tousiours eü bien de l'amour pour l'ordre que Dieu auoit estably dans son église, il m'auoit fait prier de venir pour remmetre son âme et sa conscience entre ses mains, puisque j'estois son pasteur...."

Beurrier did not advise a fresh general confession in his actual state of health of body and soul.

"Il me repartit à cela qu'il y auoit deux ans qu'il auoit fait une retraitte spirituelle, et une confession générale fort exacte, en suitte de laquelle il auoit entièrement changé de vie et pris résolution de fuir toutes les compagnies pour ne plus songer qu'à son salut," and to prepare his Apology for Christianity.

"Il me mit en suitte sur les matières du temps qui faisoient tant de bruit entre les doctes catholiques sur la doctrine de la grâce, de la puissance et authorité de pape, sur les cas de conscience et la morale chrestienne, et me dit qu'il gémissoit auec douleur de voir cette diuision entre les fidèles qui s'échauffoient si fort dans leurs disputes soit de vive voix, soit par escrit, qu'ils se décrioient mutuellement auec tant de chaleur que cela preiudicioit à l'union et à la charité qui les deuoit porter plus tost à ioindre leurs armes spirituelles contre les véritables infidèles et hérétiques que de se battre ainsy les uns les autres, m'adjoustant qu'on l'auoit voulu engager dans ces disputes, mais que depuis deux ans il s'en étoit retiré prudemment, veu la grande difficulté de ces questions si difficiles de la grâce et de la prédestination, selon l'adveu même de saint Paul qui s'écrie: o altitudo" etc. "Et, pour la question de l'autorité du pape, il l'estimoit aussi de conséquence, et très difficile à vouloir cognoistre ses bornes, et qu'ainsy n'ayant point estudié la scolastique et n'ayant eu d'austre maistre, tant dans les humanités que dans la philosophie et dans la théologie que son propre père qui l'auoit instruit et dirigé dans la lecture de la Bible, des conciles, des saints Pères, et de l'histoire ecclesiastique, il auoit iugé qu'il se deuoit retirer de ces disputes et contestations qu'il croioit præiudiciables et dangereuses, car il auroit pu errer en disant trop ou trop peu, et ainsy qu'il se tenoit au sentiment de l'Eglise touchant ces grandes questions, et qu'il vouloit auoir une parfaite soumission au vicaire de Jésus-Christ qui est le Souverain Pontife....Il adiousta que, pour ce qui est de la morale nouuelle et relâchée, qu'elle n'estoit point conforme à l'Euangile, aux canons des conciles, et aux sentimens des Pères de l'Eglise et qu'il la falloit asseurément condamner; qu'elle étoit très dangereuse parce qu'elle fauorisoit la lâcheté, le vice, le libertinage et la corruption des mœurs, qu'elle étoit très préiudiciable à l'Eglise et qu'il en auoit une très grande horreur."

It will be noticed that the words *aller trop avant* do not occur in this recital; but the sense is there.

Now it seems to me perfectly possible to reconcile the conflict of statement and opinion raised by Beurrier's recollection, and I would venture to suggest the following explanation: "Pascal, sick, weary of controversy, and sore over the Formulary, tells Beurrier in a burst of confidence what he would never have said to *ces messieurs*—that he was tired of it all; that he had better things to think of; that he did not understand the subtleties of the dispute; that he submitted his judgement to the Church. But this unburdening of his soul did not alter his outward relations with his old friends, and they, remembering what he had been to them in act and speech, protest that the expression reported by Beurrier to the Archbishop did not represent the man they knew: that he could not have uttered it; that if he said *aller trop avant* at all, he meant it of himself and not of them. Beurrier, a peaceful person, who did not know Pascal intimately (he never connected him with the Provincial

Letters), is brought to mistrust his own memory. He cannot be certain about the words, nor about their precise connotation, 'If you say he could not have said that, I suppose he did not.' But thinking the matter over quietly he is convinced of the substantial accuracy of his declaration and now tells the story over again, not without repetitions and with a naiveté which bespeaks good faith."

By some such reconstruction of the circumstances we can, I think, imagine how it all came about, and can absolve the Port-Royalists and the Periers of bad faith, while at the same time recognizing that Pascal had at the end gone further from them than they cared to contemplate or admit.

The question is discussed at length and with a different result in M. Jovy's *Pascal Inédit*, t. ii (1908), pp. 403–508, from which I have borrowed my quotations.

49 p. 17. The five Propositions—there were originally seven — which Nicolas Cornet, Syndic of the theological faculty of the University of Paris, drew from the *Augustinus* and denounced as heretical were as follows:

I. Aliqua Dei praecepta hominibus iustis volentibus et conantibus, secundum praesentes quas habent vires, sunt impossibilia; deest quoque iis gratia qua possibilia fiunt.

II. Interiori gratiae in statu naturae lapsae nunquam resistitur.

III. Ad merendum et demerendum in statu naturae lapsae, non requiritur in homine libertas a necessitate, sed sufficit libertas a coactione.

IV. Semipelagiani admittebant praevenientis gratiae interioris necessitatem ad singulos actus, etiam ad initium fidei; et in hoc erant haeretici, quod vellent eam gratiam talem esse cui posset humana voluntas resistere vel obtemperare.

V. Semipelagianum est dicere Christum pro omnibus omnino hominibus mortuum esse, aut sanguinem fudisse.

50 p. 18. Cf. Sainte-Beuve, *op. cit.* t. iii, pp. 188 ff. and t. v, *Appendice*, "Le Cardinal de Retz et les Jansénistes."

51 p. 18. "Il n'y a que la vérité qui delivre veritablement, et il est sans doute qu'elle ne delivre que ceux qui la mettent elle-mesmes en liberté en la confessant avec tant de fidelité qu'ils meritent d'estre confessez eux-mesmes et reconnus pour de vrais enfans de Dieu....Je vous demande, ma tres-chere Sœur, au nom de Dieu, dites-moy quelle difference vous trouvez entre ces deguisemens et donner de l'encens à une idole sous pretexte d'une croix qu'on a dans sa manche." Lettre de la Sœur Jacqueline de Sainte-Euphémie Pascal à la Sœur Angélique de Saint-Jean, 22, 23 June 1611. Pascal, *Œuvres*, t. x, pp. 103–112.

52 p. 19. Cf. "Je conclus que ceux qui signent purement le formulaire sans restriction, signent la condemnation de Jansénius, de St Augustin et de la grace efficace. Je conclus en second lieu que qui excepte la doctrine de Jansenius en termes formels, sauve de condemnation

et Jansénius, et la grace efficace. Je conclus en troisiesme lieu que ceux qui signent en ne parlant que de la foy, n'excluant pas formellement la doctrine de Jansénius, prennent une voye moyenne, qui est abominable devant Dieu, mesprisable devant les hommes, et entierement inutile à ceux qu'on veut perdre personellement." Pascal, *Écrit sur la signature*, *Pensées et Opuscules*, pp. 239–243; *Œuvres*, t. x, pp. 171–175.

53 p. 19. Cf. "Si un homme disoit: *Le plus grand Géometre de Paris est l'homme du monde le plus désagréable dans la conversation*, je soutiens qu'alors, comme il auroit été nécessaire que celui qui auroit parlé de la sorte, eût eu dans l'esprit une personne particuliere, qu'il auroit désignée par ces mots, de plus grand Géometre de Paris, parce qu'il ne convient point à un Géometre, comme Géometre, d'être désagréable dans la conversation, ce ne seroit point par la vérité des choses qu'on devroit juger de celui qu'il auroit estimé être désagréable dans la conversation, mais par l'opinion de cette personne. De sorte que si je savois d'ailleurs que cette personne ou ne connût pas M. Pascal, ou l'eût en estime d'un homme d'un entretien fort agréable, quoique je fusse persuadé que dans la vérité, M. Pascal est le plus grand Géometre de Paris, je ne croirois point que cet homme eût mal parlé de M. Pascal. Mais si je connoissois Roberval et que je susse que cette personne le connoît aussi, je croirois sans peine que c'est de lui qu'il a voulu parler, quelque inférieur que je le crusse à M. Pascal dans la science de la Géometrie: et le jugement que je porterois de cette Proposition est, qu'elle seroit vraie dans le fond, parce qu'il n'auroit pas mal jugé de la personne qu'il auroit eue dans l'esprit; mais qu'elle seroit fausse dans l'attribution qu'il auroit faite à cette personne, d'être le plus grand Géometre de Paris." Arnauld, *Œuvres Complètes*, t. xxii, p. 770; cf. Strowski, *op. cit.* t. iii, p. 365.

The passage is worth quoting as an example of Arnauld's subtlety and style of humour, and incidentally for the side-light which it throws on Roberval's character and reputation.

54 p. 19. "Lorsque M. Paschal fut tout à fait remis, Madame Perier lui ayant demandé ce qui lui avoit causé cet accident, il répondit: 'Quand j'ai vu toutes ces personnes-là, que je regarde comme ceux à qui Dieu a fait connoître la verité et qui doivent en être les défenseurs, s'ébranler, je vous avoue que j'ai été si saisi de douleur que je n'ai pu la soutenir, et il a fallu succomber." *Recueil d'Utrecht*, pp. 324, 325.

55 p. 19. The history of these Letters may be read in the *Recueil d'Utrecht*, pp. 317 ff., and in greater detail in the Préface historique to tome xxi of Arnauld's *Œuvres*, pp. cxxix–cxli. There Nicole tells us that after the *Écrit sur la signature* (see above, note 52)

"il se fit encore, de part et d'autre, divers écrits, dont le succès fut que chacun demeura dans ses sentiments."

He summarizes Pascal's Letters as follows:

"M. Pascal...appréhendoit que ce ne fût le desir de conserver la Maison de Port-Royal qui eût réduit ces Messieurs à ce qu'il appelloit du nom de relâchement, et qui les eût portés à ces condescendances, qu'il ne pouvoit approuver. Il crut même que ce n'étoit pas seulement dans cette occasion de la signature des filles de Port-Royal qu'on avoit paru peu sincere; mais qu'on pourroit encore trouver le même défaut dans les divers Ecrits qui avoient été faits dans la suite de l'affaire qui troubloit la paix de l'Eglise depuis si longtemps: qu'on avoit eu égard en écrivant à l'utilité présente, et que, comme elle avoit changé selon les divers temps, les Ecrits ne paroissoient pas tout-à-fait conformes. Ainsi il lui sembla qu'il eût été à propos de les revoir tous, et de les réduire à une parfaite conformité d'expressions. Pour y exciter plus fortement MM. de Port-Royal, il fit un autre Ecrit; dans lequel il prétendoit leur faire l'avantage qu'ils donnoient à leurs ennemis par cette diversité, et qu'on les pourroit convaincre d'avoir parlé plus foiblement depuis les Bulles, qu'auparavant."

He proceeds to detailed criticism, beginning with the opinion

"que M. Pascal n'ayant pas fait l'Ecrit dont il s'agit pour être publié, et tout son but n'étant que de représenter ce que l'on auroit pu dire, et le tour fâcheux que l'on pourroit donner à certaines choses, il ne s'étoit pas mis en peine d'y garder une forte grande exactitude; et que, sans consulter lui-même les Ecrits dont il tiroit des preuves de ce qu'il avançoit, ce qui lui eût été fort difficile dans la foiblesse où il étoit, qui le rendoit presque incapable de lire, il se contenta des Mémoires que lui fournissoient quelques uns de ses amis, qui ne regardoient pas d'assez près aux passages dont ils les composoient. Ainsi, quoique l'adresse de son esprit à mettre les choses dans leur jour paroisse dans cet Ecrit, comme dans tous ses autres ouvrages, comme il n'est pas possible que l'ouvrier, quelque habile qu'il soit, supplée au défaut de la matière, il n'a pu éviter de tomber dans un assez grand nombre de méprises, dont il ne sera pas inutile de marquer ici quelques causes principales."

This he proceeds to do, reaffirming at the close of his examination that Pascal's object was

"plutôt de représenter la manière dont un homme, plus habile que les Jésuites, pourroit tourner les choses, que non pas celle dont un homme sincere les doit entendre. Et c'est pourquoi il a toujours tenu cet Ecrit secret: et il avoit même ordonné à ses amis de le supprimer."

56 p. 20. "M. Pascal avoit confié tous ses écrits en mourant à M. Domat, en le priant *de les brûler si les Religieuses de Port-Royal se soutenoient, et de les faire imprimer si elles plioient*. Et comme Dieu les soutint, il est à présumer qu'on suivit ses intentions." Arnauld, *Œuvres*, t. xxi, p. cxl.

57 p. 20. Cf. *Vie de M. Pascal.*

58 p. 20. See above, note 48.

59 p. 21. He wrote to the Queen, Anne of Austria:

"La régence de votre fils ne doit pas être moins vigoureuse à étouffer ce monstre." Cf. Jovy, *op. cit.* t. iv, p. 17.

60 p. 21. Cf. *Vie de M. Pascal.*

61 p. 21. When Beurrier learnt that Pascal was the author of the *Lettres Provinciales*, he asked him whether he was sorry to have written them. Pascal replied:

"Comme étant sur le point d'aller rendre compte à Dieu de toutes ses actions, que sa conscience ne lui reprochoit rien, et qu'il n'avoit eu dans la composition de cet ouvrage aucun mauvais motif, ne l'ayant fait que pour l'intérêt de la gloire de Dieu et la défense de la vérité, sans y avoir jamais été poussé par aucune passion contre les Jésuites." *Recueil d'Utrecht*, p. 330.

62 p. 23. Cf. Letter to Madame de Grignan, 15 January, 1690.

Boileau's defence of Pascal on this occasion does more credit to his heart than to his head. When the Jesuit, "'tout rouge, tout étonné,' remarked 'Pascal est beau autant que le faux peut l'être,' Boileau exclaimed 'Le faux, le faux! Sachez qu'il est aussi vrai qu'il est inimitable; on vient de le traduire en trois langues.' Le Père répond: 'Il n'en est pas plus vrai.' Despréaux s'échauffe, et criant comme un fou: 'Quoi, mon Père, direz-vous qu'un des vôtres n'a pas fait imprimer dans un de ses livres qu'un Chrétien n'est pas obligé d'aimer Dieu? Osez-vous dire que cela est faux?' 'Monsieur,' dit le Père en fureur, 'il faut distinguer.' 'Distinguer,' dit Despréaux, 'distinguer, morbleu, distinguer, distinguer, si nous sommes obligés d'aimer Dieu!' et prenant Corbinelli par le bras s'enfuit au bout de la chambre," etc.

Five years later Boileau wrote his twelfth *Épître*, "Sur l'amour de Dieu," addressed to the Abbé Renaudot, the famous Orientalist.

63 p. 24. The *Collège de Clermont*, the principal Jesuit college in Paris, now *Collège Louis-le-grand*.

64 p. 24. Cf. "Comme nous estions tous dans l'impatience de sçavoir qui en étoit l'Inventeur, nous escrivimes à Rome," etc. Letter to Monsieur de Ribeyre, 12 July 1651. *Œuvres*, t. ii, pp. 478–495.

65 p. 24. *Le plein du vide* (1648), dedicated with a singularly fatuous preface to the Prince de Conti, and immediately afterwards translated by the author under the title *Plenum experimentis novis confirmatum auctore Stephano Natale societatis Jesu* (1648). Cf. Strowski, *op. cit.* t. ii, pp. 105 ff.; Sainte-Beuve, *op. cit.* t. ii, p. 475.

66 p. 24. Cf. "Lettre de M. Pascal le père au R. P. Noël" (1648). *Œuvres*, t. ii, pp. 255–279. "Lettre de Pascal à M. Le Pailleur au sujet du P. Noël, Jésuite" (1648) *ad fin.* *Œuvres*, t. ii, pp. 179–211.

67 p. 25. Cf. "Hanc experientiam totidem verbis D. Pascal filius Gallice exposuit in libro quem sic inscripsit, *Experiences nouvelles touchant le vuide*. In quo, et singularem ab omnibus gratiam iniit, et magnam ipse ingenii, et doctrinae, laudem assequutus est." *Plenum*, p. 2.

The eulogy is absent from the French treatise, which simply states that Pascal has made the experiment.

68 p. 25. Cf. *Lettre de M. Pascal le fils adressante à M. le Premier Président de la Cour des Aydes de Clermont-Ferrand*

sur le subjet de ce qui s'est passé en sa présence dans le collège des Jésuites de Montferrand aux thèses de philosophie qui luy ont esté dédiées et qui ont esté soubtenuës le 25 *juin* 1651. Pascal, *Œuvres*, t. ii, pp. 478 ff. The passage of which Pascal complains is the following:

"Il y a certaines personnes aymans la nouveauté, qui se veulent dire les Inventeurs d'une certaine experience dont Toricelli est l'Auteur, qui a esté faite en Pologne; et non obstant cela, ces personnes se la voulans attribuer, après l'avoir faicte en Normandie, sont venues la publier en Auvergne."

69 p. 25. Cf. Strowski, *op. cit.* t. ii, p. 179.

70 p. 25. Cf. "Et comme je suis certain que Galilée et Toricelli eussent esté ravis d'apprendre de leur temps qu'on eut passé outre la cognoissance qu'ils ont euë, je vous proteste, Monsieur, que je n'auray jamais plus de joye que de voir que quelqu'un passe outre que celle que j'ay donnée." Letter to Ribeyre, *l.c.* p. 495.

71 p. 25. Cf. "C'est moy qui l'avois prié, il y a 2 ans de la vouloir faire (l'experience), et je l'avois assuré du succez, comme estant entierement conforme à mes principes, sans quoy il n'eust eu garde d'y penser, à cause qu'il étoit d'opinion contraire." Descartes, Letter to Carcavi, 17 August 1649.

72 p. 26. Cf. "Encore que personne ne soit obligé d'estre sçavant non plus que d'estre riche, personne n'est dispensé d'estre sincere: de sorte que le reproche de l'ignorance n'a rien d'injurieux que pour celuy qui le profere; mais celuy de larcin est de telle nature, qu'un homme d'honneur ne doit point souffrir de s'en voir accusé, sans s'exposer au peril que son silence tienne lieu de conviction." Second letter to M. de Ribeyre, 8 August 1651, *Œuvres*, t. ii, pp. 500–502.

73 p. 26. E.g. V. Cantor, *Vorlesungen über die Geschichte der Mathematik* (1892), Bd ii, p. 807. Maximilien Marie, *Histoire des sciences mathématiques*, t. iv, s.v. Torricelli.

74 p. 27. Cf. "De Trochoide...sive Italicum sive Gallicum problema sit, nihil mea interest: meum certe non est quod ad inventionem attinet ......ex improviso quando nil tale sperabam nuncius horribilis ex vobis affertur haec omnia ante me vos etiam invenisse. Si verum hoc est, certe pro meis illa amplius non essent habenda," etc. Gröning, *Historia Cycloeidis* in *Bibliotheca Universalis* (1701), t. i, pp. 34 ff.

75 p. 27. It has been suggested with a good deal of probability that the *Histoire de la Roulette*, which contains the attack on Torricelli's memory, was written from Roberval's notes, if not in great part by Roberval's own hand. See Stuyvaert, *Bibliotheca Mathematica*, 3rd series, vol. 8, pp. 170–172.

76 p. 27. Forty pistoles for the earliest solution received, twenty for the second; sixty if there was only one solution. The pistole = a louis = 11 fr.

According to Marguerite Perier it was the Duc de

Roannez who suggested the challenge to Pascal as a useful instrument in his work of confuting the unbelievers:

"Que dans le dessein où il étoit de combattre les athées, il falloit leur montrer qu'il en savoit plus qu'eux tous en ce qui regarde la geometrie et ce qui est sujet à la démonstration ; et qu'ainsy s'il se soumettoit à ce qui regarde la foy, c'est qu'il savoit jusques où devoient porter les demonstrations." Pascal, *Œuvres*, t. i, p. 135.

This apologetic motive, if it was the true one, perhaps explains Pascal's want of generosity to his rivals.

77 p. 27. Cf. Tannery, P., *Mémoires de la Soc. des Sciences physiques et naturelles de Bordeaux*, 3e série, t. v (1890), pp. 55–84, and 4e série, t. iv (1894), pp. 251–259; Bertrand, J., *Journal des Savants* (1890), pp. 320–329; Maximilien Marie, *Histoire des sciences mathématiques*, t. vi, s.v. Wallis.

78 p. 27. Cf. Tannery, *op. cit.* pp. 70, 84. For a different opinion on Lalouvère and Pascal's behaviour towards him, see Jovy, *op. cit.* i, pp. 473 ff.

79 p. 28. Arnauld's father, a celebrated barrister, pleaded in the name of the University of Paris against the Jesuits in 1594, on the occasion of Barrière's attempt against Henry IV. His language was of a kind to rankle:

"Boutique de Satan où se sont forgés tous les assassinats qui ont été exécutés ou tentés en Europe depuis quarante ans ; ô vrais successeurs des Arsacides ou assassins !" etc.

The Jesuits were the great schoolmasters of the day, and the Jansenists had recently established at Port-Royal *Les petites écoles* on a system fundamentally opposed to theirs. Cf. Tilley, *From Montaigne to Molière*, p. 226.

80 p. 28. Not Calvin, who in these matters simply codified Luther's doctrines, and did not penetrate to Louvain until a later date. Cf. J. Paquier, *Le Jansénisme* (1909), p. 126.

81 p. 28. Cf. *Wider die xxxii Artikel der Teologisten von Löwen* (1545).

82 p. 28. See *Biographie Nationale de Belgique*, s.v. De Bay.

83 p. 29. Cf. J.-B. du Chesne, *Histoire du Baianisme* (1731), p. 209.

84 p. 29. *ib.* p. 210.

85 p. 29. Cf. "Familiaribus quandoque fassus est, se decies et amplius universa opera Augustini, attentione acri, adnotatione diligenti, libros vero contra Pelagianos facile trigesies a capite ad calcem evolvisse." *Synopsis vitae auctoris*, prefixed to the *Augustinus*.

86 p. 29. In the Bull, *In eminenti*, § 8, of 6 March 1641. See Paquier, *op. cit.* p. 160.

87 p. 29. Cf. "Quae (principia) si data explanataque semper fuissent, forte neque Pelagiana haeresis fuisset exorta: neque Lutherani tam impudenter arbitrii nostri libertatem fuissent ausi negare, obtendentes cum divina gratia, praescientia, et praedestionatione cohaerere non posse; neque ex Augustini opinione concertationibusque cum Pelagianis, tot fideles fuissent turbati ad Pelagianosque defecissent," etc. *Concordia Liberi arbitrii* (1588), *In quaest.* xxiii, *art.* IV and V, *Disp.* I, *membr. ult.*

88 p. 29. Cf. Arnauld, *Œuvres*, t. xvi, p. 250.

89 p. 30. *La Fréquente Communion* is contained in t. xxvii of the *Œuvres*; *La Théologie morale des Jésuites* in t. xxix.

90 p. 30. Mme de Sablé and the Princesse de Guemené. The former was at this moment under Jesuit direction. For sketch of this volatile lady see above, p. 9.

91 p. 30. See above, note 79.

92 p. 31. See Arnauld, *Considérations sur l'entreprise du Sieur Cornet*. Arnauld, *Œuvres*, t. xix.

93 p. 31. Cf. "Je crois que les Propositions sont véritablement dans Jansénius et qu'elles sont l'âme de son livre." Bossuet, *Œuvres*, ed. Lebel, t. xxxvii, p. 125.

94 p. 31. Roger du Plessis, Duc de Liancourt, converted to Jansenism and moral living by his excellent wife, was charged in January 1665 by a priest of St-Sulpice, M. Picoté, of having a Jansenist in his house and a granddaughter at Port-Royal. The Duke could not deny the facts and would not utter the *mea culpa* required of him, so M. Olier, *curé* of St-Sulpice, refused him absolution. Hence Arnauld's Letters, the Sorbonne's censure, and, ultimately, the *Provincial Letters.*

95 p. 31. *Lettre...à une Personne de Condition sur ce qui est arrivé depuis peu, dans une paroisse de Paris, à un seigneur de la Cour*, 24 January 1653, Arnauld, *Œuvres*, t. xix, pp. 311–334. *Lettre...à un Duc et Pair de France*, 10 July 1653, *ib.* pp. 338–558.

96 p. 31. Cf. "Croirons nous que S. Augustin a reconnu, que jamais une grâce actuelle et suffisante ne manque aux justes, lorsqu'il a dit de S. Pierre: *qu'il suivit le Seigneur qui alloit souffrir la mort: mais qu'alors il ne le put suivre en souffrant la mort: qu'il avoit promis de mourir pour lui et qu'il ne put même mourir avec lui; parce qu'il avoit plus entrepris que ses forces ne pouvoient: qu'il avoit plus promis qu'il ne pouvoit accomplir* (de divers. serm. 106, c. 1)? Quand il dit encore du même apôtre *qu'il n'auroit pas renoncé Jesus Christ, si Jesus Christ ne l'eût abandonné pour un temps, et qu'il n'auroit pas pleuré sa faute, si Jesus Christ ne l'eût regardé* (Hom. 4, inter. 11 ultimas). Et quand il dit enfin: *que l'homme sans la grâce de Dieu, est ce que fut S. Pierre, lorsqu'il renonça*

Jesus Christ; et que c'est pour cette raison que le Sauveur abandonna S. Pierre pour un peu de temps, à fin que tous les hommes pussent reconnoître, par son exemple, qu'ils ne peuvent rien sans la grâce de Dieu (Serm. 124 de temp.). A-t-il voulu par ces paroles...que jamais aucun juste...ne manque de la grâce intérieure qui lui est nécessaire pour pouvoir vaincre toutes sortes de tentations, lorsqu'il dit, au contraire, que S. Pierre en a manqué: que Dieu l'avoit abandonné en cette rencontre; *qu'il ne pouvoit* s'exposer a mourir pour Jesus Christ: qu'il n'avoit pas des forces capables de lui faire mépriser la mort, et que tous les hommes doivent voir, dans la chûte du Chef de l'Église, privé du secours de la grâce, qu'ils ne peuvent rien sans la grâce?" Arnauld, *Œuvres*, t. xix, pp. 528, 529.

97 p. 32. The Dominicans are called Thomists after their most illustrious member, St Thomas, and Jacobins after the church of Saint-Jacques, near which they had their monastery.

The Molinists are the followers of Luis Molina, a Spanish Jesuit (1535–1601), professor of theology at Evora in Portugal. In the course of composing his commentary on the *Summa* (pub. 1593) the idea came to him of that reconciliation of Freedom and Predestination to which he has given his name. This was expressed in his *De liberi arbitrii cum gratiae donis concordia* (1588), in which he supposes a Grace which is efficacious or not according to the co-operation or resistance of the human will. His theory was violently assailed by the Spanish Dominicans in the name of St Thomas, by the Calvinists, and later by Jansen. The case between the Dominicans and him was carried to Rome and debated under three Popes for ten years (1597–1607) in the celebrated congregation *De Auxiliis*. No decision was reached, and Paul V forbad further public dispute on the question. How well he was obeyed is shown by the story of these Lectures. Bossuet, who was equally opposed to Jansenism and Molinism, defends the latter from the charge of semi-Pelagianism in his *Deuxième Avertissement aux Protestants*; *Œuvres*, ed. Lebel, t. xxi, p. 133.

98 p. 33. For "proximate power," see below, note 101.

99 p. 35. Cf. *Augustinus*, t. iii, "De gratia Christi Salvatoris," *passim*, and especially the following passages:

"*Tertio*, delectationem istam caelestem esse verum ex Augustini sensu medicinalis gratiae adiutorium, quod Deus ad iustitiam operandam voluntati tribuit, ex eo demonstrari potest, quia similiter docet, delectationem terrenam esse causam cur ab Adami posteris iustitia deseratur, ac deserendo peccetur." lib. iv, c. iii.

"Quarto itaque demonstrari potest, suavitatem illam caelestem verum illud Christi adiutorium: quo iuvamur ad non peccandum, recteque faciendum, quia creberrime docet Augustinus, quamdiu in hac vita mortali vivimus, esse in homine luctam quandam duarum delectationum, noxiae et beneficae, terrenae atque caelestis: quarum utralibet vicerit, animum secum consentientem ac pronum trahit." *ib.* c. iv.

"Ex his iam perspicue intelligitur, tantopere esse necessariam istam Delectationis divinae gratiam, quando cum terrenarum rerum tentationibus ac delectationibus dimicamus, ut nisi maior fuerit quam terrena, qua noster affectus detinetur, fieri non possit quin propriae voluntatis infirmitate vincamur." *ib.* c. vi.

"Sicut ergo non voluit (Apostolus) voluntatem Dei ad salutem omnium omnino hominum extendi, sed illorum dumtaxat, qui ex omni gente et lingua, ex omni nominum genere praedestinati sunt: ita nec voluit effectus istius voluntatis, hoc est mortem, sanguinem, redemptionem, propitiationem, orationem Christi ad omnes homines dilatari, sed vel ad solos illos qui praedestinati sunt." *ib.* lib. iii, c. xx, *ad fin.*

"Quid ergo, si haec ita sint, insulsius et ineptius, quam hominibus peccata sua contra Dei querelas excusantibus, quod ab ipso excoecati atque obdurati, et a gratia deserti sunt, per quae suppliciosa, fatente docenteque hoc Aug. tam impotentes ad bene vivendum facti sunt, ut ne quidem videre possint quod eligendum est, bonum, *voluntatemque* habeant *durissimam, et adversus Deum omnino inflexibilem*; talibus, inquam, excusationibus nihil aliud Dei conquerentis patrocinio proferre, quam Gratiam esse quae subtrahitur, iustamque peccatorum poenam quae infligitur?...Deficit enim profecto et Apostolus et Augustinus, si Deo de peccatis hominum conquerente et homine identidem responsante, Deum abstulisse sibi gratiam sine qua peccata vitare non potuit, clamat solummodo *o homo tu quis es qui respondeas Deo? voluntati enim eius quis resistit?*" *ib.* lib. iii, c. xiv.

100 p. 35. By "proximate power" the Thomists meant an inward virtue which only passes into action when it is called forth by efficacious grace; the Molinists on the other hand meant by it a power which lacks nothing necessary for action. Alvarez, archbishop of Trani, the founder and leader of the Neo Thomists, seems to have been the first to use the term in his *De Auxiliis Divinae Gratiae* (1610), *Disput.* i and ii, where he clearly distinguishes the two notions:

"Potentia potest dupliciter dici proxima, et expedita ad operandum. Primo; quia nihil aliud requiritur ex parte ipsius potentiae, quo in actu primo constituatur ad actualiter operandum, sive ad volendum, et nolendum; et hoc modo liberum arbitrium, positis omnibus requisitis ad operandum, potest potentia proxima et expedita operari et non operari, velle et nolle...secundo modo potest dici facultas vel potentia proxima et expedita ad operandum, quia in sua operatione non dependet ab alia priori causa efficienter ei tribuente ipsum cooperari, vel actualiter concurrere; et in hoc sensu nulla causa secunda, quantumvis ponatur perfecta, est secundum se, et seclusa praemotione divina, expedita ad operandum quia ut supra dictum est ex S. Thoma, nulla causa secunda quantumvis perfecta potest in suum actum prodire nisi virtute motionis divinae."

101 p. 36. All this attempted discrimination between the rival systems of Grace is founded upon the admirably clear account by C.-L. Montagne (1687–1767), in his *Tractatus de Gratia* (Migne, *Theologiae cursus completus*, t. x); cf. esp. *Pars dogmatica*, lib. iii, *De gratia efficaci*, col. 980–1062.

A passage between the redoubtable Dominican Thomas de Lemos and one of the five Jesuit opponents whom he demolished in the Conferences *De Auxiliis*, gives in a nutshell the respective Molinist and Thomist views of *gratia sufficiens*:

"Gratia quae dat vires ut possimus est gratia sufficiens: sed gratia sufficiens est vera gratia: ergo Pelagius, qui secundum te admisit gratiam quae dat ut possimus, agnovit etiam veram gratiam. *Rursus* secundum S. Augustinum ex tua expositione, gratia quae dat tantum posse, non est vera gratia: sed auxilium sufficiens dat tantum posse: ergo sequitur ex tua responsione quod auxilium sufficiens non sit vera gratia. Respondit semel et iterum Thomas de Lemos: Gratiam, quae veri nominis gratia est, vereque sufficiens, non eam esse quae dat posse tantum extrinsecum, excitando, invitando et alliciendo; qualem Pelagius et Molina noverunt: sed illam quae intrinsecam et supernaturalem potentiam elargitur. Quanquam nec illa etiam vera Christi gratia putanda sit quae datur electis secernitque bonos a malis: haec enim non solum dat posse quod volumus, sed etiam velle et operari quod possumus." Cf. Serry, *Hist. Congreg. de Auxiliis*, lib. iii, c. 28. Cf. also Montagne, *op. cit.* col. 298.

102 p. 37. "C'est à dire, leur dis-je en les quittant (the Dominicans and Molinists), qu'il faut prononcer ce mot des lévres de peur d'estre heretique de nom. Car enfin est-ce que le mot est de l'Ecriture? Non, me dirent-ils. Est-il donc des Peres, ou des Conciles, ou des Papes? Non. Est-il donc de saint Thomas? Non. Quelle necessité y a-t-il donc de le dire, puisqu'il n'a ny authorité ny aucun sens de luy-mesme? Vous estes opiniastre, me dirent-ils; vous le direz, ou vous serez heretique, et Monsieur Arnauld aussi. Car nous sommes le plus grand nombre, et s'il est besoin, nous ferons venir tant de Cordeliers que nous l'emporterons." i[e] *Provinciale.*

Pascal's Parthian shot is a pun on the precious test-word:

"Je vous laisse cependant dans la liberté de tenir pour le mot de *prochain* ou non; car j'aime trop mon prochain pour le persecuter sous ce pretexte."

103 p. 37. Cf. "Mais apres tout, mon Pere (a Dominican), à quoy avez-vous pensé de donner le nom de suffisante à une grace que vous dites, qu'il est de foy de croire qu'elle est insuffisante en effet? Vous en parlez, dit-il, bien à vostre aise. Vous estes libre et particulier: je suis religieux et en communauté. N'en sçavez-vous pas peser la difference? Nous dépendons des Superieurs. Ils despendent d'ailleurs. Ils ont promis nos suffrages: que voulez-vous que je devienne?" iie *Provinciale.*

104 p. 37. Cf. "Laissons donc là leurs differens. Ce sont des disputes de Theologiens et non pas de Theologie. Nous qui ne sommes point Docteurs n'avons que faire à leurs démeslez." iiie *Provinciale.*

105 p. 38. Arnauld, *Seconde Apologie de Jansenius*, ch. xiv–xix, of which the theme as announced is:

"Que c'est une vérité indubitable dans la doctrine de S. Augustin; que toutes les actions des Infideles sont péchés; et qu'elle est principalement établie sur ces deux maximes. L'une; que nulle action ne peut être bonne, si elle n'est faite par un mouvement d'amour de Dieu. L'autre; que les Infideles ne peuvent faire aucune action par un mouvement d'amour de Dieu." *Œuvres*, t. xvii, p. 303.

106 p. 38. Cf. Sainte-Beuve, *op. cit.* t. iii, p. 102, Strowski, *op. cit.* t. iii, p. 85.

107 p. 38. "White heat" is not an exaggerated expression for the pace at which the first two letters were written. But it is a common mistake to suppose that the First was ready the day after Arnauld's suggestion. What Nicole says in his Preface to the third edition (1660) of his translation of the *Letters* is that Pascal began to work at it the very next day.

"Postridie cum eandem illam, quam promiserat, informationem vellet ordiri, primam epistolam, qualis typis vulgata cernitur, uno impetu ac tenore perfecit."

We learn from Charles Perrault that a week elapsed before it was printed (*Mémoires*, ed. Bonnefon, 1909, p. 29).

The Second *Letter* took six days and the Third eleven to prepare and publish. After that the period of composition varies between ten days (*Letter* xii) and sixty days (*Letter* xviii).

108 p. 38. "Mes Reverends Peres, mes Lettres n'avoient pas accoustumé de se suivre de si pres, ny d'estre si etenduës. Le peu de temps que j'ay eu a esté cause de l'un et de l'autre. Je n'ay fait celle-cy plus longue que parceque je n'ay pas eu le loisir de la faire plus courte." L. P. xvi. xvie *Provinciale.*

109 p. 39. Cf. "Mais, mon Pere, luy dis-je, on doit estre bien embarrassé a choisir alors! Point du tout, dit-il, il n'y a qu'à suivre l'avis qui agrée le plus. Et quoy si l'autre est plus probable? Il n'importe, me dit-il. Et si l'autre est plus seur? Il n'importe, me dit encore le Pere: le voyci bien expliqué. C'est Emmanuel Sa de nostre Societé. *On peut faire ce qu'on pense estre permis selon une opinion probable, quoy que le contraire soit plus seur. Or l'opinion d'un seul Docteur grave y suffit.*" v[e] *Provinciale.* Pascal's quotation is exact. Cf. "Potest quis facere quod probabili ratione vel auctoritate putat licere, etiamsi oppositum tutius sit: sufficit autem opinio alicuius gravis Doctoris, aut bonorum exemplum." Emmanuel Sà (1530–1596), *Aphorismi Confessoriorum* (Douai 1618), p. 190, *s.v.* "Dubium."

110 p. 39. The theory known as Probabilism was first propounded in set terms by the Spanish Dominican, Bartolomé de Medina (1528–1581), in his Exposition of St Thomas.

Cf. "Si opinio est probabilis, licet eam sequi, licet opposita probabilior sit; nam opinio probabilis in speculativis ea est quam possumus sequi sine periculo erroris et deceptionis, ergo opinio probabilis in practicis ea est quam possumus sequi sine periculo peccandi." *Expos. in I Secundae D. Thomae* (1580), *qu.* xix *art.* vii.

But "nihil nocet," the constant refrain of the Penitentials, was clearly opening the way to some such theory and to a wide extension of the field of *ἀδιάφορα*. The casuistical *Summae* carried the matter still further; thus the *Summa angelica* (1486) of Angelus de Clavasio and the *Summa Rosella* (1495) of Baptista Trovamala are dictionaries of moral problems together with their various solutions and the authorities which supply them. E.g.:

"Joannes Andreae dicit quod quamquam hec opinio probabilis, tutius tamen istius (sc. Papae) requiratur consilium," *S. Rosella*, s.v. "consilium."

111 p. 40. Cf. *Theologia Moralis*, i, bk 2, § 1, ch. I quoted by Nicole, *Morale des Jesuites*, i, 334.

112 p. 40. Cf. *Blaise Pascal*, by Father G. O'Neill, S. J. (1902), Cath. Truth Society.

113 p. 40. Cf. Strowski, *op. cit.* t. iii, pp. 121 ff.

114 p. 41. "Scachez donc que leur objet n'est pas de corrompre les Mœurs: ce n'est pas leur dessein: Mais ils n'ont pas aussi pour unique but celuy de les reformer. Ce seroit une mauvaise politique. Voicy quelle est leur pensée. Ils ont assez bonne opinion d'eux-mesmes pour croire qu'il est utile et comme necessaire au bien de la Religion que leur credit s'estende partout, et qu'ils gouvernent toutes les consciences." v[e] *Provinciale*.

115 p. 41. See Parkman, F. *The Jesuits in North America*, esp. ch. ix.

Maffei, G. P. *Rerum a Soc. Jesu in Oriente gestarum volumen* (1574).

Darde, J. *Hist. de ce qui s'est passé en Éthiopie, Malabar, Brasil et es Indes orientales* (1628).

Satow, E. M. *Mission Press in Japan* (1888).

And in general, Crétineau-Joly, J., *Hist. de la congrégation de Jésus*, 5 vols. (1884–5).

116 p. 42. The admission, which I readily make, that the *Lettres Provinciales* helped to effect a change in Jesuit practice, does not invalidate my contention that Jesuit principles remained the same. Arnauld writes in 1686 that

Jesuit preachers now advise a delay of absolution for mortal sins, and Bourdaloue deserves the title given him by Sainte-Beuve, "le plus Janséniste des Jésuites," for his insistence on the need of worthy Reception. Bourdaloue saw, what many of his brethren did not see, the danger of the "demi-christianisme" with which they were content; and his eyes were doubtless opened by Jansenist thoroughness. But he was only giving a new application to the principles of Ignatius Loyola, of which the foremost was the sanctification of the servants of Christ that they might sanctify the world. That Jesuits both before Bourdaloue and since have worked their principles differently does not affect those principles any more than bad arguments impair a sound conclusion.

117 p. 42. Cf. The *Ante-Nicene Fathers* (1895), pp. 105 ff.

118 p. 44. See Salmon, *Papal Infallibility* (ed. 1890), p. 430.

119 p. 44. See Bull, *Pascendi Gregis*: "On the doctrine of the Modernists." See Paquier, *op. cit.* p. 180.

120 p. 45. "Ne vous imaginez pas...que les lettres du Pape Zacharie pour l'excommunication de S. Virgile, sur ce qu'il tenoit qu'il y avoit des antipodes, ayent aneanti ce nouveau monde; et qu'encore qu'il eust declaré que cette opinion estoit une erreur bien dangereux, le Roy d'Espagne ne se soit pas bien trouvé d'en avoir plûtost crû Christofle Colomb qui en venoit, que le jugement de ce Pape qui n'y avoit pas esté." xviiie *Provinciale.*

"Ce fut aussi en vain que vous obtintes contre Galilée ce Decret de Rome, qui condamnoit son opinion touchant le mouvement de la terre. Ce ne sera pas cela qui prouvera qu'elle demeure en repos; et, si l'on avoit des observations constantes qui prouvassent que c'est elle qui tourne, tous les hommes ensemble ne l'empescheroient pas de tourner, et ne s'empescheroient pas de tourner aussi avec elle." *ib.*

121 p. 46. "Un tres petit nombre de personnes, qui font à toute heure des petits escrits volans, disent que ce fait est de sa nature separé du droit....Mais comme ces deux mots ne se regardent que dans nos entretiens, et dans quelques escrits tout à fait separez des constitutions, lesquel peuvent perir, et la signature subsister" etc. *Écrit sur la Signature*, *Œuvres*, t. x, pp. 171–175.

122 p. 46. Cf. "Graces à Dieu je n'ay d'attache sur la terre qu'à la seule Eglise Catholique Apostolique et Romaine, dans laquelle je veux vivre et mourir, et dans la communion avec le Pape son souverain Chef, hors de laquelle je suis tres-persuadé qu'il n'y a point de salut." xviie *Provinciale.*

"Je ne me separeray jamais de sa communion, au moins je prie Dieu de m'en faire la grace; sans quoy je serois perdu pour jamais." Letter to Mlle de Roannez, *Œuvres*, t. vi, p. 217.

123 p. 47. Cf. Sainte-Beuve, *op. cit.* t. iii, pp. 374, 376.

124 p. 48. Cf. Sainte-Beuve, *op. cit.* t. vi, ch. XIII.

125 p. 49. Forming tomes xii–xiv of *Œuvres de Pascal*, in the series of "Grands Écrivains Français."

126 p. 49. See a fine passage in V. Giraud's *Blaise Pascal*, pp. 109 ff. ending:

"Assurément il ne suffit pas, pour bien parler de Pascal, d'avoir vu et étudié son écriture; mais il semble pourtant qu'à contempler ses brouillons, on entre mieux dans la familiarité de son génie et dans l'intimité de son âme."

127 p. 50. To him was entrusted the composition of the Preface to the volume. For some reason or other it did not satisfy the Periers, who quietly suppressed it and substituted one by Étienne. See Sainte-Beuve, *op. cit.* t. iii, pp. 386 ff. Filleau's account was however published in 1672 under the title *Discours sur les Pensées de M. Pascal où l'on essaie de faire voir quel était son dessein* par M. Dubois de la Cour.

128 p. 51. See above, note 48.

129 p. 51. For the history of the Sainte Épine see Sainte-Beuve, *op. cit.* t. iii. pp. 76, 174–180.

130 p. 51. "M. Pascal avoit accoutumé, quand il travailloit, de former dans sa teste tout ce qu'il vouloit escrire sans presque en faire de projet sur le papier; et il avoit pour cela une qualité extraordinaire, qui est qu'il n'oublioit jamais rien, et il disoit luy mesme qu'il n'avoit jamais rien oublié de ce qu'il avoit voulu retenir." *Mémoire sur la vie de M. Pascal écrit par Mlle Marguerite Perier sa nièce.* Pascal, *Œuvres*, t. i, pp. 125–136.

131 p. 52. See just above, note 127. M. Brunschvicg accords less trust to Filleau's *Discours* than does M. Strowski. See *Œuvres*, t. xii, pp. liii ff. and Strowski, *op. cit.* t. iii, 286 ff. I venture to follow M. Strowski in believing it to be a veracious account of Pascal's exposition.

132 p. 53. *Grammar of Assent*, p. 281.

133 p. 54. Cf. "Qu'on se mette à la place d'un homme que M. Pascal supposoit avoir du sens...on verra sans doute qu'il n'est pas possible qu'il ne vienne ensuite à s'effrayer de ce qu'il découvrira en lui, et à se regarder comme un assemblage monstrueux de parties incompatibles...qu'enfin ces mouvements involontaires du cœur qu'il condamne...ne le démontent, et ne lui fassent douter qu'une nature si pleine de contrarietés, et double et unique tout ensemble, comme il sent le sienne, puisse être une simple production du hasard, ou être sortie telle des mains de son auteur." *Discours sur les Pensées de M. Pascal.* See above, note 127.

134 p. 54. "Que trouve-t-il dans cette recherche? Des religions qui commencent avec de certains peuples, et finissent avec eux; des religions où l'on adore plusieurs dieux, et des dieux plus ridicules que les hommes, des religions qui n'ont rien de spirituel, ni d'élevé, qui autorisent le vice, qui s'établissent tantôt par la force, et tantôt par la fourberie; qui sont

sans autorité, sans preuve, sans rien de surnaturel; qui n'ont qu'un culte grossier et charnel, où tout est extérieur, tout sentant l'homme, tout indigne de Dieu, et qui le laissant dans la même ignorance de la nature de Dieu et de la sienne, ne font que lui apprendre de plus en plus jusqu'où peut aller l'extravagance des hommes. Enfin, plutôt que d'en choisir aucune, et d'y établir son repos, il prendroit le parti de se donner lui-même la mort, pour sortir, tout d'un coup, d'un état si misérable, lorsque, près de tomber dans le désespoir, il découvre un certain peuple," etc. *Discours.*

135 p. 55. "Mais cependant il se présente d'abord une difficulte qui paroît insurmontable; et au même temps qu'on voit clairement que si c'est un Dieu qui a créé les hommes, et qu'il ait lui-même rendu témoignage de la bonté de ses ouvrages, il faut que l'homme ait été dans l'état que j'ai dit: on se sent si éloigné de cet état que l'on ne sait plus où l'on en est." *Discours.*

136 p. 57. "N'est ce pas encore ici en quoi ce Livre est aimable et digne qu'on s'y attache? Non-seulement il est le seul qui a bien connu la misère des hommes; mais il est aussi le seul qui leur ait proposé l'idée d'un vrai bien, et promis des remedes apparens à leurs maux. S'il nous abat en nous faisant voir notre état plus déplorable encore qu'il ne nous paroissoit, il nous console aussi, en nous apprenant qu'il n'est pas désespéré. Il nous flatte peut-être; mais la chose vaut bien la peine de l'expérimenter: et le bonheur qu'il promet réveille au moins nos espérances....Mais ce qu'il y a de plus considérable, c'est qu'ils (ceux qui ont travaillé a ce Livre) nous apprennent que ces remedes ne sont point dans nos mains....Ils nous avertissent que c'est à Dieu que nous devons demander ces forces qui nous manquent." *Discours.*

137 p. 57. "Que ce système est beau, quoi qu'on en puisse dire, et qu'il est conforme aux apparences et à la raison même, autant qu'elle y peut avoir de part!...Il ne faut que voir ce qu'ont dit les plus habiles de ceux qui ont voulu discourir sur ce sujet, ou d'eux mêmes, ou après avoir vu les livres de Moïse, pour juger que cela n'est pas marqué au coin des hommes." *Discours.*

138 p. 57. "Mais...qu'ils se fassent justice; et que par le peu d'assurance qu'ils trouvent en eux, pour juger les moindres choses, ils se reconnoissent incapables de décider par eux-mêmes...et qu'enfin ils s'estiment heureux de ce qu'en une chose qui les touche de si près, au lieu d'être à la merci de cette pauvre raison, à qui il est si aisé d'imposer, ils n'ont à examiner pour toutes preuves, que des faits et des histoires, c'est-à-dire, des choses pour lesquelles ils ont des principes infaillibles." *Discours.*

139 p. 58. Richard Simon (1638–1712), Oratorian, the father of Biblical criticism, incurred the resentment of Port-Royal by his criticisms of Arnauld's *Perpétuité de la Foi* and the censure of Bossuet and violent opposition of the Protestants by his *Histoire critique du Vieux Testament.* He had to leave the Oratory and retired to his *cure* in Normandy, dying at Dieppe, where he is buried.

140 p. 58. "Quand il n'y auroit point de prophéties pour Jésus-

Christ, et qu'il seroit sans miracles, il y a quelque chose de si divin dans sa Doctrine et dans sa vie, qu'il en faut au moins être charmé ; et que, comme il n'y a ni véritable vertu ni droiture de cœur sans l'amour de Jésus-Christ, il n'y a non plus ni hauteur d'intelligence ni délicatesse de sentiment sans l'admiration de Jésus-Christ....Que Socrate et Epictete paroissent, et qu'au même temps que tous les hommes du monde leur céderont pour les mœurs, ils reconnoissent eux-mêmes que toute leur justice et toute leur vertu s'évanouit comme une ombre et s'anéantit devant celle de Jésus-Christ....Il n'y a que les disciples de Jésus-Christ qui sont dans l'ordre de la justice véritablement universelle, et qui, portant leur vue dans l'infini, jugent de toutes choses par une règle infaillible, c'est-à-dire, par la justice de Dieu....A en juger sainement, il n'est pas moins au-dessus de l'homme de vivre comme il a vécu et comme il veut que nous vivions, que de ressusciter les morts et de transporter les montagnes." *Discours.*

141 p. 58. "Que ceux...que cette vie divine ne touchera pas s'examinent à la rigueur; ils trouveront assurément que la difficulté qu'ils ont à croire ne vient que de celle qu'ils auroient à obéir; et que si Jésus-Christ s'étoit contenté de vivre comme il a fait, sans vouloir qu'on l'imitât, ils n'auroient nulle peine à le regarder comme un objet digne de leurs adorations. Mais au moins que cela leur rende leurs doutes suspects; et s'ils connoissent bien le pouvoir du cœur et de quelle sorte l'esprit en est toujours entraîné, qu'ils se regardent comme juges et parties; et que pour en juger équitablement ils essaient d'oublier pour un temps le malheureux interêt qu'ils peuvent y avoir. Autrement il ne faut pas qu'ils s'attendent de trouver jamais de lumière; la dureté de leur cœur résistera toujours aux preuves de sentiment, et jamais les autres ne pourront rien sur les nuages de leur esprit." *Discours.*

142 p. 59. "Il est sans doute que toutes les vérités sont éternelles, qu'elles sont liées et dépendantes les unes des autres; et cet enchaînement n'est pas seulement pour les vérités naturelles et morales, mais encore pour les vérités de fait....Ainsi si les hommes n'avoient point l'esprit borné et plein de nuages, et que ce grand pays de la vérité leur fût ouvert et exposé tout entier à leurs yeux, comme une province dans une carte de géographie, ils auroient raison de ne vouloir rien recevoir qui ne fût de la dernière évidence, et dont ils ne vissent tous les principes et toutes les suites. Mais puisqu'il n'a pas plu à Dieu de les traiter si avantageusement...il faut qu'ils agissent au moins raisonnablement dans l'étendue de leur capacité bornée, sans se réduire à l'impossible, et se rendre malheureux et ridicules à la fois." *Discours.*

143 p. 59. "Car enfin il n'a pas prétendu donner de la foi aux hommes, ni leur changer le cœur." *Discours.*

144 p. 59. On the *Pari* (*Pensées*, no. 233) see É. Boutroux, *Pascal*, in the series "Grands Écrivains français," pp. 178 ff.

"Tous les hommes se haissent naturellement l'un l'autre." *Pensées*, no. 451.

145 p. 59. "Les hommes sont si nécessairement fous que ce serait estre fou par un autre tour de folie de n'estre pas fou." *Pensées*, no. 414.

"Le dernier acte est sanglant quel que belle que soyt la comedie en tout le reste: on jette enfin de la terre sur la teste, et en voilà pour jamais." *Pensées*, no. 210.

146 p. 60. *Pensées*, no. 553.

147 p. 60. Cf. "Mais quoy qu'il eut un tres grande probité...on peut dire que tout ce qu'il faisoit n'estoit proprement l'effet que d'une vertu morale, mais point du tout d'une vertu chrestienne." Marguerite Perier on her grandfather before his conversion. See Pascal, *Œuvres*, t. i, p. 16.

148 p. 60. Contrast Augustine, *Confess.* v. 13 and 14 with *Confess.* VIII. 12.

149 p. 61. "Il vouloit sçavoir la raison de toutes choses...il a eu toujours une netteté d'esprit admirable pour discerner le faux; et on peut dire que tousjours et en toutes choses la verité a esté le seul objet de son esprit, puisque jamais rien n'a sceu et n'a pû le satisfaire que sa connoissance. Ainsy des son enfance, il ne pouvoit se rendre qu'à ce qui luy paroissoit vray evidemment; de sorte que, quand on ne lui donnoit pas de bonnes raisons, il en cherchoit luy mesme; et quand il s'estoit attaché à quelque chose, il ne la quittoit point qu'il n'en eust trouvé quelqu'une qui le pust satisfaire." *Vie de M. Pascal.*

150 p. 61. On the monk, Saint-Ange, and his hazardous theology see Strowski, *op. cit.* t. i, pp. 208 ff.

151 p. 62. PASCAL'S "MEMORIAL."

See reduced facsimile in *Œuvres*, t. iv.

L'an de grace 1654.
Lundy 23 novembre, jour de St Clement, pape
et martir et autres au martiloge
veille de St Chrysogone martir, et autres
Depuis environ dix heures et demy du soir jusques environ minuit
et demy
Feu
Dieu d'Abraham, Dieu d'Isaac, Dieu de Jacob
Non des philosophes et des scavans
Certitude Certitude Sentiment Joye Paix
Dieu de Jesus Christ
Deum meum et Deum vestrum
Ton Dieu sera mon Dieu.
Oubly du monde et de tout, hormis Dieu.
Il ne se trouve que par les voyes enseignées dans l'Evangile
Grandeur de l'ame humaine.
Pere juste, le monde ne t'a point connu, mais je t'ay connu
Joye, joye, joye, pleurs de joye
Je m'en suis separé.
Dereliquerunt me fontem aquae vivae
Mon Dieu me quitterez-vous?
Que je n'en sois pas separé eternellement

Cette est la vie eternelle qu'ils te connoissent seul vray

Dieu et celuy que tu as envoyé J. C.
Jesus Christ
Jesus Christ
Je m'en suis separé; je l'ai fuy renoncé crucifié
Que je n'en sois jamais separé
Il ne se conserve que par les voies enseignées dans l'Evangile.
Renontiation totalle et douce
Soûmission totale à Jesus Christ et à mon directeur.
Eternellemt en joye pour un jour d'exercice sur la terre.
Non obliviscar sermones tuos. Amen.

The last three lines "Soûmission" etc. are not in the autograph MS. preserved in the *Bibliothèque nationale*, but the copy made by Pascal's nephew, the Abbé Perier, has them (with a note stating that they were indistinct), and they probably figured in the original parchment which Perier claims to have copied exactly.

M. Strowski shews convincingly that Pascal had before him a copy of the translation of Lefèvre d'Étaples. See *op. cit.* t. ii, p. 356 *n.*

152 p. 63. Cf. "C'est le cœur qui sent Dieu, et non la raison. Voila ce que c'est que la foy, Dieu sensible au cœur, non à la raison." *Pensées*, no. 278.

"La raison agit avec lenteur, et avec tant de vues, sur tant de principes, lesquels il faut qu'ils soient toujours presens, qu'à toute heure elle s'assoupit et s'egare, manque d'avoir tous ses principes presens. Le sentiment n'agit pas ainsi, il agit en un instant, et toujours est pret à agir. Il faut donc mettre notre foi dans le sentiment, autrement elle sera toujours vacillante." *Pensées*, no. 252.

"Nous connoissons la verité non seullement par la raison, mais encore par le cœur, c'est de cette derniere sorte que nous connoissons les premiers principes, et c'est en vain que le raisonnement, qui n'y a point de part, essaie de les combattre.... Car la cognoissance des premiers principes, comme qu'il y a *espace*, *temps*, *mouvement*, *nombres*, [*est*] aussy ferme qu'aucune de celles que nos raisonnemens nous donnent. Et c'est sur ces cognoissances du cœur et de l'instinct qu'il faut que la raison s'appuie, et qu'elle y fonde tout son discours." *Pensées*, no. 282.

153 p. 64. See above, note 100.

154 p. 64. Cf. "Ita tamen quod a sola gratia coeptum est pariter ab utroque perficitur ut mixtum non singillatim; simul non vicissim, per singulos profectus operentur. Non partim gratia partim liberum arbitrium, sed totum singula opere individuo peragunt. Totum quidem hoc et totum illa; sed ut totum in illo, sic totum ex illa." St Bernard, *Tract. de gratia et libero arbitrio*, c. xiv.

155 p. 66. Cf. "On peut être un peu surpris...d'entendre un Ecrivain aussi rempli de lumiere que l'étoit M. Nicole avancer que les infideles pourroient faire, qu'ils faisoient même quelquefois, en vertu de la seule Grace générale, *des actions exemptes de tout péché*, que ces actions *étoient rapportées à Dieu*, que dans certaines occasions les

infideles aimoient *la sagesse pour elle-même*, qu'ils étoient *capables de quelque amour de Dieu pour lui-même et de n'aimer point la créature dans quelque action*; que comme l'amour dominant de Dieu dans les Justes n'est point incompatible avec des degrés d'amour de la créature pour elle-même, mais non dominant, de même l'amour dominant de la créature ' tel qu'il est dans le cœur des infides, n'est point incompatible avec une infinité de degrés d'amour de Dieu plus foibles, et qui ne justifient point, mais qui sont néanmoins des amours de Dieu pour lui-même, des mouvements qui se rapportent à Dieu, qui demeurent en Dieu, et qui par conséquent sont exempts de déréglement et de péché, parce que ce sont des mouvements par lesquels les hommes *fruuntur Deo, non creatura.*' " Arnauld, *Œuvres*, t. x, p. xxviii.

156 p. 66. *De la nécessité de la foi en Jésus-Christ pour être sauvé* (1641: first published in 1701). *Œuvres*, t. x, pp. 65 ff.

157 p. 66. The story of Nicole's defection, which is of capital importance in the history of Jansenism and for a proper understanding of Pascal's experience, may be read in the "Discours préliminaire" to his *Traité de la Grace générale*; in the tenth volume of Arnauld's works; and in M. Jovy's *Pascal Inédit*, t. ii, pp. 362–402.

What led him away from Jansenism towards Thomism was a desire to mitigate the harshness ("un air de dureté, un certain air farouche") with which the former expressed the doctrine of St Augustine. "Feu M. Pascal avec qui j'ai eu le bien d'être tres étroitement uni, n'a pas peu aidé à nourrir en moi cette inclination." His first attempt was made in connexion with the *Provincial Letters*, viz. the *Disquisitiones Pauli Irenaei*, and the *Willelmi Wendrockii dialogus Epistolae decimae octavae illustrandae serviens*, which he appended to his translation into Latin of the series.

From that date (1657) onwards his new ideas were ventilated in manuscript tracts, and even crept into the fourth volume of his *Essais de Morale*. When Arnauld got wind of these variations—it must be remembered that Nicole, the Melanchthon of Port-Royal, was peaceful and timid and kept as much as possible out of print—he published several strong remonstrances (among others an *Écrit géometrique sur la Grâce !*). He considered that Nicole was imperilling sound theology and plunging deep into error.

Another detailed criticism of Nicole's system is also contained in J.-J. Duguet's *Lettre sur la Grâce* (1718) which is printed in the same volume with Arnauld's writings.

Duguet, a Jansenist of the second generation and a close friend of Quesnel's, deeply regrets Nicole's lapse into Molinism ("M. Nicole est tombé dans le Molinisme") and his indifference to the opinion of St Augustine. "Je ne sais," he had said, "si St Augustin les a admises (grâce générale + grâce efficace). Je n'ai aucun sentiment ni pour ni contre. Je prétends seulement qu'on ne sauroit démontrer par la Raison la fausseté de l'opinion qui les admet." But Nicole remained unmoved. He died in 1695 without recanting his conviction that the heathen were not of necessity sinful in all their actions, that they were accessible to God's grace, and to the benefits bestowed by a Redeemer who died for all men. Which is not Jansenism.

158 p. 66. Cf. "Auxquels des Molinistes, me dit-il, me renvoyez-vous? Je les luy offris tous ensemble comme ne faisant qu'un mesme corps et n'agissant que par un mesme esprit." i[e] *Provinciale.*

"Ainsi Mon Pere vos adversaires sont parfaitement d'accord avec les nouveaux Thomistes mesmes: puisque les Thomistes tiennent comme eux et le pouvoir de resister à la grace et l'infaillibilité de l'effet de la grace qu'ils font profession de soutenir si hautement." xviiie *Provinciale.*

In the Eighteenth Letter he quotes Alvarez, the Dominican, as stating the doctrine of St Augustine and St Thomas: he actually claims the support of Petau, the great Jesuit, against Calvin for the freedom to resist grace if one will. He traces the line of orthodox Augustinian doctrine from St Augustine through St Thomas to the new Thomists, whereas Jansen calls the latter disciples of Aristotle rather than of Augustine ("magis profecto Aristotelici quam Augustiniani sunt") and devotes much space to the distinction between his doctrine of *gratia efficax* and their *praedeterminatio physica.* See "De Gratia Christi salvatoris," lib. ix, in *Augustinus*, tom. iii.

Finally, he is as anxious to maintain against Calvin the power of the Will to resist Grace as he is to maintain against Molina the power of the Grace over the Will—"aussi jaloux de l'une de ces vérités que de l'autre."

159 p. 67. For instance, in his very effort to establish the identity of the teaching of Jansen with that of St Augustine and St Thomas and its difference from that of Calvin (see last note), he allows his zeal to master his judgement. It is the main theme of the Eighteenth Letter, and it reposes, as Mozley in his *Augustinian Doctrine of Predestination* pointed out, upon a fallacy. Pascal claims that Jansen admitted, while

Calvin denied, the "power of resisting"; in other words that Jansen believed and Calvin did not believe in Free Will. But in Augustine's (and Jansen's) *potestas resistendi* there is always present the qualification *si vult.* And Calvin was at one with them here. "All that the Augustinian and Jansenist admission with respect to free will amounts to is the admission of a *will* in man, and this admission Calvin is equally ready to admit." He never denied that man had the power to resist grace if he will. What he maintained was that man cannot will to resist it for it is Grace itself which determined his Will. See Mozley, *op. cit.* note xxi.

160 p. 67. (1) *Lettre touchant la possibilité d'accomplir les commandements de Dieu.*

(2) *Dissertation sur le véritable sens de ces paroles: Les commandements ne sont pas impossibles aux justes.*

(3) *Discours où l'on fait voir qu'il n'y a pas une relation nécessaire entre la possibilité et le pouvoir.*

These pieces owe their title to their first editor Bossut (1779), who while recognizing their theological value treated them somewhat cavalierly. They were first printed in their entirety, together with some other unpublished fragments, by M. E. Jovy in *Pascal Inédit*, t. i (1908), and have since been incorporated in the edition of the "Grands Écrivains Français." *Œuvres*, t. xi, pp. 95–295.

161 p. 67. "En cet état, où nous regardons la volonté humaine, on voit bien qu'elle n'a rien en elle-même, qui l'applique à une chose plutôt qu'à l'autre, que sa propre détermination"; Bossuet, *Traité du Libre Arbitre* (Lebel's edition, t. xxxiv, p. 447), in which he openly espouses Thomism in preference to Jansenism and Molinism. "Tel est le sentiment de ceux qu'on appelle Thomistes." *Ib.* p. 434. "Cette manière de concilier le libre arbitre avec la volonte de Dieu, paroit la plus simple." *Ib.* p. 447.

162 p. 68. "Voilà les sujets de crainte et d'espérance qui doivent animer continuellement les saints: et c'est pourquoi, suivant saint Augustin, Jésus-Christ voulut, étant à la croix, donner un insigne exemple de l'un et de l'autre, dans l'abandonnement de saint Pierre sans grace, et dans la conversion du Larron par un prodigieux effet de grace. C'est en cette sorte que tous les hommes doivent toujours s'humilier sous la main de Dieu en qualité de pauvres, et dire comme David: Seigneur, je suis pauvre et mendiant." Jovy, *op. cit.* t. i, p. 100.

163 p. 68. See above, note 48.

164 p. 68. "L'homme n'est pas digne de Dieu, mais il n'est pas incapable d'en estre rendu digne." *Pensées*, no. 510.

"Il se découvre à ceus qui le cherchent, parce que les hommes sont tout ensemble indignes de Dieu, et capables de Dieu; indignes par leur corruption, capables par leur premiere nature." *Pensées*, no. 557.

"Ainsi il y a deux natures en nous, l'une bonne et l'autre mauvaise. Où est Dieu? Où vous n'estes pas, et le Royaume de Dieu est dans vous." Molinier, t. i, p. 295.

"Dieu délivrera la bonne nature de l'homme de la mauvaise." *Pensées*, no. 446.

"Pour faire d'un homme un saint, il faut bien que ce soit la grace; et qui en doute, ne sait ce que c'est que saint et qu'homme." *Pensées*, no. 508.

165 p. 68. "Le monde subsiste pour exercer misericorde et jugement, non pas comme si les hommes y etoient sortant des mains de Dieu, mais comme les ennemis de Dieu, auxquels il donne, par grace, assez de lumiere pour revenir s'ils le veulent chercher et le suivre, mais pour les punir, s'ils refusent de le chercher ou de le suivre." *Pensées*, no. 584.

166 p. 69. "Il y a donc sans doute une presomption insupportable dans ces sortes de raisonnemens, quoi qu'ils paroissent fondés sur une humilité apparente, qui n'est ni sincere ni raisonnable, si elle ne nous fait confesser que, ne sachant de nous mesmes qui nous sommes, nous ne pouvons l'apprendre que de Dieu." *Pensées*, no. 430.

167 p. 69. "Je ne vous separe point vous deux, et je songe sans cesse à l'un et à l'autre." Letter of 5 November 1656. The Letters to the Roannez are contained in *Pensées et Opuscules*, pp. 209–224, and in *Œuvres*, tomes v and vi.

168 p. 69. "Il est bien assuré qu'on ne se détache jamais sans douleur. On ne sent pas son bien quand on suit volontairement celuy qui entraisne. Mais quand on commence à resister et à marcher en s'éloignant, on souffre bien. Le bien s'étend et endure toute la violence." Letter of 24 September 1656, *Œuvres*, t. v, p. 409.

169 p. 70. She married the Duc de La Feuillade in 1667, and died after a series of misfortunes in 1683. Cf. Strowski, *op. cit.* iii, p. 152.

170 p. 71. "Dieu veut plus disposer la volonté que l'esprit. La clarté parfaite serviroit à l'esprit et nuiroit à la volonté." *Pensées*, no. 581.

171 p. 71. "Je puis bien aymer l'obscurité totale: mais si Dieu m'engage dans un estat à demy obscur, ce peu d'obscurité qui y est me deplaist, et parce que je n'y vois pas le merite d'une entiere obscurité, il ne me plaist pas. C'est un defaut, et une marque que je me fais une idole de l'obscurité, separee de l'ordre de Dieu. Or il ne faut adorer que son ordre." *Pensées*, no. 582.

172 p. 72. Cf. Lavisse, E., *Histoire de France* (1906), t. vii, pp. 91 ff.

173 p. 73. Cf. Lancelot, *Mémoires de M. Saint-Cyran* (left in MS. but published 1738), t. i, p. 39.

174 p. 73. "Je ne veux point de douleur qui se répande dans les sens: prenez garde à vos larmes. Je ne veux point de mines, de soupirs ni de gestes, mais un silence d'esprit qui retranche tout mouvement." Letter to Sister Marie-Claire (Arnauld) *ap.* Sainte-Beuve, *op. cit.* t. i, p. 350.

175 p. 73. Arnauld d'Andilly, an elder brother of the great Arnauld, is at first sight an exception to the rule of Jansenist severity. He joined the *Solitaires* in 1646, aged 57, after a life of brilliant success in the world. But even after his retirement he kept up external relations to an extent which justifies the statement that he was "not a regular member of the community" (Tilley, *From Montaigne to Molière*, p. 224). He was an enthusiastic gardener and his pears were much appreciated by the Queen, to whom he presented specimens.

176 p. 74. When Saint-Cyran learnt that Richelieu was intending an appeal to Rome for help in suppressing the *Augustinus*, he said,

"S'il fait cela, nous lui ferons voir autre chose. Quand le Roi et le Pape se ligueraient ensemble pour ruiner ce livre, ils n'en viendraient jamais à bout." See Lavisse, *op. cit.* p. 92.

The spirit of independence disclosed by this passage is enough to account for the antipathy of Louis XIV against the Jansenists, whom he mistrusted on political as well as religious grounds, regarding them as an obstacle to all order and unity.

177 p. 74. Cf. "Il n'y a plus d'Église, et cela depuis plus de cinq ou six cents ans...maintenant ce qui nous semble l'Église ce n'est plus que bourbe." Saint-Cyran to M. Vincent.

178 p. 74. See H. T. Morgan, *Port Royal* (1914).

179 p. 74. Cf. "Le sacerdoce est un mystère aussi terrible que le sacrement qui en est le principal effet." Saint-Cyran, *Lettres chrétiennes* (ed. 1744), t. ii, p. 454.

"Je sçay le respect que je dois à MM. les Evesques, mais ma conscience ne me permet pas de signer qu'une chose est dans un livre où je ne l'ay pas veüe...Mais peut estre on nous retranchera de l'Eglise? Mais qui ne sçait que personne n'en peut estre retranché malgré soy, et que, l'Esprit de Jesus-Christ estant le lien qui unit ses membres à luy et entre eux, nous pouvons bien estre privez des marques, mais non jamais de l'effet de cette union, tant que nous conserverons la charité....Puis que les Evesques ont des courages de filles, les filles doivent avoir des courages d'Evesques." Jacqueline Pascal on the Formulary, 22 June 1661. See Pascal, *Œuvres*, t. x, pp. 103 ff.

According to Saint-Cyran the church is not a monarchy but an aristocracy, ruled by the bishops. But while with one hand he raises the bishops to the level of the Pope, with the other he raises the parish priest to equality with the bishop.

"Nam Parochorum officium, si minus institutionis divinae seorsum in se est at est in Episcopo; non solum quia ab Episcopo sit institutum, ut alia quaevis episcopalia instituta; sed quia in Episcopo inclusum a Christo est, ut in fonte ac plenitudine Ecclesiasticae et Hierarchicae potestatis, cuius Parochialis potestas est decidua pars, ab Episcopo in Parochum ut a fonte in rivum transfusa, sine detrimento tamen aut imminutione...

Itaque Ministrorum potestas (de potestate iurisdictionis agimus...) sic ab Episcopo fluens divinae est non humanae institutionis, quia eadem rivi est, quae fontis natura, eadem vis causae principalis, et instrumenti eadem Ministrorum regiorum et regis potestas." *Petrus Aurelius* (i.e. Saint-Cyran), t. ii (ed. of 1646), p. 226.

Similarly it is not the water of Baptism alone that makes the Christian:

"Nomen enim Christiani unctionem Spiritus sancti sequitur cum eaque pari passu ambulat; non autem ab externa ceremonia pendet, multo minus in ea sita est." *Petrus Aurelius*, t. i, p. 28.

The *Petrus Aurelius* has a special interest for English readers in that it was written by Saint-Cyran (and his friends?) to defend episcopal jurisdiction against the English Jesuits who objected to the pretensions of William Bishop, titular bishop of Chalcedon, with rights over England (1623). See Stillingfleet, *Discourse concerning...idolatry* (1709), ch. iv, 162 ff. See also Reuchlin, *Geschichte von Port-Royal* (1839), vol. i, pp. 378–411, and Bayle, *Dictionnaire critique*, s.v. "Knot."

Saint-Cyran expresses the same sentiments freely in his *Lettres chrétiennes*, e.g.

"Il n'y a que lui seul (Dieu) qui puisse donner des Prêtres à son Eglise, tant par son élection, que par l'ordination." *Lettres chrétiennes*, t. i, p. 160.

"Dieu nous a fait voir qu'outre l'onction Episcopale il faut une élection divine pour la Prêtrise, que Dieu se l'est réservée, et que l'Evêque s'y peut tromper." *ib.* t. ii, p. 346.

"Il faut que le Saint-Esprit repose sur quelqu'un pour le faire Prêtre et qu'ensuite il soit consacré." *ib.* p. 400.

"La Grace du Baptême...conduit comme d'elle même...au Sacerdoce qu'on peut nommer en un sens la fin et la perfection de la Grace du Baptême." *ib.* t. i, p. 144.

Elsewhere he contrasts the "vraie vocation venue du ciel" with the "vocation extérieure et pour ainsi dire de la terre." *ib.* p. 157.

180 p. 74. Cf. "Il n'y a pas d'idée plus terrible que celle de Dieu." Saint-Cyran, *Lettres chrétiennes*, t. i, p. 107.

181 p. 75. See above p. 30.

182 p. 75. "Et j'ose dire qu'il y a des âmes, qui étant revenues de l'état du péché, dans lequel elles avoient passé plusieurs années sont tellement touchées par un mouvement de la grâce et par l'esprit de pénitence, qu'elles seroient ravies de pouvoir témoigner à Dieu la douleur et le regret qui leur reste de l'avoir offensé en différant leur communion jusques à la fin de leur vie." Arnauld, *Œuvres*, t. xxvii, p. 89. Cf. "Il faudroit sçavoir qu'elle n'est donnée que pour médecine, et non proprement pour nourriture à la plûpart des ames." Saint-Cyran, *Lettres chrétiennes*, t. ii, p. 742.

183 p. 75. "Quelle vanité que la peinture, qui attire l'admiration

par la ressemblance des choses dont on n'admire point les originaux." *Pensées*, no. 134.

"Tous les grands divertissemens sont dangereux pour la vie chrestienne, mais entre tous ceux que le monde a inventez, il n'y en a point qui soit plus à craindre que la commedie. C'est une representation si naturelle et si delicate des passions, qu'elle les emeut et les fait naistre dans notre cœur, et surtout celle de l'amour," etc. *Pensées*, no. 11.

183 p. 75. See "L'invention Mathématique," ch. iii of H. Poincaré's *Science et Méthode* (1900), pp. 43 ff., for an account by a man of science of the process by which scientific discovery is made: see especially a remarkable passage in H. v. Helmholtz's speech on the occasion of his 70th birthday:

"Da ich aber ziemlich oft in die unbehagliche Lage kam auf günstige Einfälle harren zu müssen, habe ich darüber, wann und wo sie mir kamen, einige Erfahrungen gewonnen, die vielleicht Anderen noch nützlich werden können. Sie schleichen oft genug still in den Gedankenkreis ein, ohne dass man gleich von Anfang ihre Bedeutung erkennt; dann hilft später nur zuweilen noch ein zufälliger Umstand zu erkennen, wann und unter welchen Umständen sie gekommen sind; sonst sind sie da, ohne dass man weiss woher. In anderen Fällen aber treten sie plötzlich ein, ohne Anstrengung, wie eine Inspiration. So weit meine Erfahrung geht, kamen sie nie dem ermüdeten Gehirne und nicht am Schreibtisch...oft waren sie...des Morgens beim Aufwachen da...Besonders gern aber kamen sie...bei gemächlichem Steigen über waldige Berge in sonnigen Wetter." He adds "Die kleinsten Mengen alkoholischen Getränks aber schienen sie zu verscheuchen." *Aussprachen und Reden...zu Ehren von H. von Helmholtz* (1892), p. 55.

184 p. 76. "Il faut se mettre à la place de ceux qui doivent nous entendre, et faire essai sur son propre cœur du tour qu'on donne à son discours, pour voir si l'un est fait pour l'autre, et si l'on peut s'assurer que l'auditeur sera comme forcé de se rendre. Il faut se renfermer, le plus qu'il est possible, dans le simple naturel; ne pas faire grand ce qui est petit, ni petit ce qui est grand. Ce n'est pas assez qu'une chose soit belle, il faut qu'elle soit propre au sujet, qu'il n'y ait rien de trop ni rien de manqué." *Pensées*, no. 16.

185 p. 76. "C'estoit une faute sur laquelle on ne s'examinoit pas assez, qui avoit de grandes suittes, et qui estoit d'autant plus à craindre qu'elle nous paroist souvent moins dangereuse." *Vie de Blaise Pascal.* It should be noted that the extraordinary definition of marriage in a letter to Mme Perier (1659), "C'est une espèce d'homicide et comme un déicide," is not his own but that of *ces messieurs*, quoted, it is true, by him with apparent approval. See *Pensées et Opuscules*, pp. 227, 228.

186 p. 77. "Il est injuste qu'on s'attache à moy, quoy-qu'on le fasse avec plaisir et volontairement. Je tromperois ceux à qui j'en ferois naistre le desir, car je ne suis la fin de personne et n'ay pas de quoy les satisfaire. Ne suis je pas prest à mourir? et ainsy l'objet de leur attachement mourra. Donc comme je serois coupable de faire croire une fausseté, quoyque je le persuadasse doucement, et qu'on la crut avec plaisir et qu'en cela on me fit plaisir, de mesme je suis coupable de me

faire aymer, et si j'attire les gens à s'attacher à moy. Je dois avertir ceux qui seroient prests à consentir au mensonge, qu'ils ne doivent pas croire, quelque avantage qui m'en revint, et de mesme qu'ils ne doivent pas s'attacher à moy, car il faut qu'ils passent leur vie et leurs soings à plaire à Dieu ou à le chercher." *Pensées*, no. 471. The words are indeed touching testimony to the real warmth of Pascal's affections which he feared would tie him to earth and keep him from God, who claimed his whole being. This lesson he learned from Saint-Cyran who, writing about his own nephews, says "Je ne tiens nullement aux hommes et ne veux pas que les hommes tiennent les uns aux autres; je veux qu'ils tiennent à Dieu, et eux et moi, et que nous allions à yeux clos, où il nous appelle." *Lettres chrétiennes*, t. ii, p. 554.

187 p. 77. Cf. *Lettres, Opuscules et Mémoires de Madame Perier et de Jacqueline, sœurs de Pascal, et de Marguerite Perier, sa nièce*, published by P. Faugère (1845). Marguerite's stories have to be strictly controlled. See Strowski, *op. cit.* t. i, p. 464 *n.*

188 p. 78. Cf. "Lorsqu'on le luy vouloit représenter, particulièrement lorsqu'il faisoit quelque aumosne considérable, il en avoit de la peine et nous disoit: 'J'ay remarqué une chose, que quelque pauvre qu'on soit on laisse tousjours quelque chose en mourant.' Il a esté quelque fois si avant, qu'il a esté reduit de s'obliger pour vivre et de prendre de l'argent à rente, pour avoir donné aux pauvres tout ce qu'il avoit, et ne voulant pas aprez cela recourir à ses amis."

"Il avoit tousjours eu un si grand amour pour la pauvreté qu'elle luy estoit continuellement presente; de sorte que, des qu'il vouloit entreprendre quelque chose, ou que quelqu'un luy demandoit conseil, la premiere pensée qui luy montoit du cœur à l'esprit, estoit de voir si la pauvreté pouvoit y estre pratiquée,...Il disoit encore que la frequentation des pauvres estoit extremement utile, par ce que, voiant continuellement la misere dont ils sont accablez, et que souvent mesme ils manquent des choses les plus necessaires, il faudroit estre bien dur pour ne pas se priver volontairement des commoditez inutiles et des ajustements superflus." *Vie de M. Pascal.*

189 p. 78. Cf. "On m'a congratulée pour la grande ferveur qui vous eleve si fort au-dessus de toutes les manieres communes, que vous mettez les balais au rang des meubles superflus." Jacqueline to Blaise, 1 December, 1655. Pascal, *Œuvres*, t. iv, p. 81.

A second hand in one MS., not appreciating Jacqueline's irony and humour, gives "valets" for "balais," in support of which reading a reference to "la personne qui vous sert" lower down in the same letter has been quoted. See Victor Cousin, *Jacqueline Pascal*, p. 197. After all, it is only a question of more or less slovenliness.

190 p. 79. Cf. "Il disoit que nous n'estions pas appelez au general mais au particulier; et qu'il croyoit que la maniere de servir les pauvres la plus agreable à Dieu estoit de servir les pauvres pauvrement, c'est à dire selon son pouvoir, sans se remplir de ces grands desseins qui tiennent de

cette excellence dont il blamoit la recherche en toutes choses," etc. *Vie de M. Pascal.*

191 p. 79. A saying of Condorcet's is quoted "Qu'il y a loin de là au traité de la Roulette!" But it must be admitted that Condorcet in his *Éloge de Pascal*, prefixed to his *Choix des Pensées*, speaks of the *ceinture de fer* with more seriousness than one might expect. He pleads "la longue mélancolie de Pascal" against those who would mock him, and adds: "d'ailleurs il n'y a rien d'extraordinaire, d'absurde même, dans les opinions ou dans la conduite qu'on ne trouvât à justifier par l'exemple de quelques grands hommes."

For another and more sympathetic view of the function of the iron girdle see A. Vinet, *Études sur Pascal* (1853), pp. 6 and 7.

192 p. 79. "Le moy est hayssable: vous, Mitton, le couvrez, vous ne l'ostez pas pour cela: vous estes donc toujours hayssable.... Mais si je le hay parce qu'il est injuste, qu'il se fait centre de tout, je le hairay toujours." *Pensées*, no. 455.

"Chacun est un tout à soy mesme, car, luy mort, le tout est mort pour soy. Et de là vient que chacun croit estre tout à tous." *Pensées*, no. 457.

193 p. 80. "Je te suis present par ma parolle dans l'Escriture, par mon esprit dans l'Eglise et par les inspirations, par ma puissance dans les prestres, par ma prière dans les fidelles." *Pensées*, no. 553, "Le Mystère de Jesus."

194 p. 80. Cf. "Il est constant que les veritables pasteurs de l'Eglise, qui sont les veritables depositaires de la parolle divine, l'ont conservée immuablement contre les efforts de ceux qui ont entrepris de la ruiner." *Pensées*, no. 889.

"L'histoire de l'Eglise doit estre proprement appelée l'histoire de la verité." *Pensées*, no. 858.

"Elle (l'Eglise) n'a pas changé d'esprit, quoiqu'elle ait changé de conduite." *Comparaison des Chrétiens des premiers temps avec ceux d'aujourd'hui. Pensées et Opuscules*, p. 202; *Œuvres*, t. x, p. 418.

195 p. 80. "Toutes les fois que les Jesuites surprendront le Pape, on rendra toute la chrestienté parjure. Le Pape est tres aisé à estre surpris à cause de ses affaires et de la creance qu'il a aux Jesuites; et les Jesuites sont très capables de surprendre à cause de la calomnie." *Pensées*, no. 882.

196 p. 81. Cf. "Et pour la question de l'authorité du Pape, il l'estimoit aussi de conséquence, et très difficile à vouloir cognoistre ses bornes, et qu'ainsy n'ayant point estudié la scolastique...il auoit jugé qu'il se deuoit retirer de ces disputes et contestations qu'il croioit præiudiciables et dangereuses, car il auoit pu errer en disant trop ou trop peu, et ainsy qu'il se tenoit au sentiment de l'Eglise touchant ces grandes questions (de la grâce et de la prédestination), et qu'il vouloit auoir une parfaite soumission au vicaire de Jésus-Christ qui est le Souverain Pontife." Jovy, *op. cit.* t. ii, p. 490.

197 p. 81. "Si mes lettres sont condamnées a Rome, ce que j'y condamne est condamné dans le ciel. *Ad tuum*," etc. *Pensées*, no. 920.

The *Provincial Letters* were placed on the *Index* on 6 September 1657; the *conseil d'état* condemned the Latin translation in September 1660.

198 p. 81. Cf. Sainte-Beuve, *op. cit.* t. iii, pp. 88, 89.

199 See above, note 48.

200 p. 82. "La bonne crainte vient de la foy, la fausse crainte vient du doute. La bonne crainte, joincte à l'esperance, parce qu'elle naist de la foy, et qu'on espere au Dieu que l'on croit: la mauvaise, joincte au desespoir, parce qu'on craint le Dieu auquel on n'a point de foy. Les uns craignent de le perdre, les autres craignent de le trouver." *Pensées*, no. 262.

201 p. 82. "Une personne me disoit un jour qu'il avoit une grande joye et confiance en sortant de confession. L'autre me disoit qu'il restoit en crainte. Je pensay sur cela, que de ces deux on en feroit un bon, et que chacun manquoit en ce qu'il n'avoit pas le sentiment de l'autre." *Pensées*, no. 530.

202 p. 82. Cf. "C'est une des choses dont il faut dire maintenant ce que S. Augustin dit de certains autres points, quod saepe dixi et quod saepe dicendum est, qu'il n'y a rien de si grand dans l'Eglise de Dieu; et il n'y a rien de si avili. Elle l'est beaucoup plus que la communion. Car on croit bien faire de parler des vérités divines dans une chaire, quand on a étudié et qu'on a le talent, comme l'on dit, de prêcher, c'est à dire, de parler facilement et en Orateur. Car pour le moins il y a peu de personnes qui communient dans certaines imperfections, qui ne reconnoissent qu'ils n'ont pas toute la préparation qu'il faudroit pour recevoir le Corps du Fils de Dieu." *Lettres chrétiennes*, t. ii, p. 743.

203 p. 83. "La conduitte de Dieu qui dispose toutes choses avec douceur, est de mettre la religion dans l'esprit par les raisons, et dans le cœur par la grace. Mais de la vouloir mettre dans l'esprit et dans le cœur par la force et par les menaces, ce n'est pas y mettre la religion, mais la terreur, *terrorem potius quam religionem*." *Pensées*, no. 185.

M. Brunschvicg sees in this *Pensée* essential Jansenism: "la conception fondamentale du Christianisme, suivant les maîtres du Jansénisme, c'est qu'il a substitué le règne de l'amour à la loi du terreur qui était la loi des Juifs." *Pensées et Opuscules*, p. 413. But it need hardly be observed that there is nothing peculiarly Jansenist in the substitution of Love for Law (cf. Jn i. 17; Rom. v, 20, 21, etc.), while a reference to the pages of Bossuet will shew that it was recognized in orthodox circles at the time; cf. *Sermon sur les deux alliances*. In his large edition M. Brunschvicg tacitly abandons the claim put forward for Jansenism and refers the reader to Grotius's *De vera religione*.

It does not seem probable that either of M. Brunschvicg's sources was in Pascal's mind when he quoted from some unknown writer, *terrorem potius quam religionem.* No doubt Jansenists were distinguished from Jesuits by the stress they laid upon Love in the process of the sinner's recovery. It is the theme of the tenth *Provincial Letter* and of Boileau's *Epistle* "Sur l'amour de Dieu." For the proper reception of the Sacrament of Penance they demanded perfect Contrition, i.e. "l'amour dominant et par lequel on aime Dieu plus que toutes choses" (Arnauld, *Œuvres*, t. iii, p. 740). The Jesuits, anxious, as always, to render religion accessible to the greatest number, only asked for Attrition, without any explicit act of love. But the insistence on Contrition was not peculiar to the Jansenists. Schoolmen taught it, Trent endorsed it (Sess. vi, cap. 6), Bossuet proclaimed it (cf. *Second Catéchisme de Meaux*, 5e partie, and constantly elsewhere). On the other hand the Jesuit opinion as to the sufficiency of Attrition with Penance was shared by many Catholic doctors; e.g. Liguori calls it "certain" (*Theol. moral.* vi, n. 440), and it is commonly held to-day. Cf. Paquier, *op. cit.* p. 393; *Catholic Dict.* (ed. 1903), s.v. Attrition.

A passage of Sainte-Beuve deserves quoting in this connexion.

"Comme M. de Saint-Cyran (et celui-ci lui en savait gré), saint François de Sales avance que l'amour de Dieu est nécessaire à l'entière pénitence, que la pénitence sans l'amour est incomplète;—oui, mais il le dit plus doucement. Il dit qu'elle est *incomplète*, et non pas *nulle*; il admet qu'elle achemine. Il n'effraie ni ne consterne en recommandant l'amour, au rebours des Jansénistes, qui le commandent avec terreur. En parlant d'Éternité, il ne met pas comme eux le marché à la main; il ne présente pas toujours dans la même phrase cette redoutable alternative: *amour* ou *damnation*. On a dit de la devise de certains révolutionnaires qu'elle revenait à ceci: *sois mon père ou je te tue*. Saint François de Sales ne tombe pas le moins du monde dans cette sorte de contradiction." *Op. cit.* t. i, p. 234.

It seems to me that Pascal is on the side of Saint François de Sales. In any case it is highly significant that the Port-Royalist editors, who had a remarkably sure instinct for what fell in with their doctrine and what did not, should have omitted this *Pensée* from their collection.

204 p. 83. Cf. "Ce n'est pas l'absolution seule qui remet les pechés au sacrement de penitence, mais la contrition, qui n'est point veritable si elle ne recherche le sacrement." *Pensées*, no. 923.

"Les anciens ont donné l'absolution avant la pénitence? Faittes-le en esprit d'exception. Mais, de l'exception, vous faittes une regle sans exception, en sorte que vous ne voulez plus mesme que la regle soit en exception." *Pensées*, no. 904.

Cf. also the whole of the *Comparaison des Chrétiens des premiers temps avec ceux d'aujourd'hui*, written under the obvious influence of *La Fréquente Communion*, e.g. "On frequente les Sacrements, et on jouit des plaisirs de ce monde, etc. Et ainsy, au lieu qu'autrefois on voyoit une distinction essentielle entre l'un et l'autre, on les voit maintenant confondus et meslez, en sorte qu'on les discerne quasi plus." *Œuvres*, t. x, p. 413 ; *Pensées et Opuscules*, p. 202.

205 p. 83. "Et enfin, quand il a voulu accomplir la promesse qu'il fit à ses Apostres de demeurer avec les hommes jusques à son dernier avenement, il a choisy d'y demeurer dans le plus estrange et le plus obscur secret de tous, qui sont les especes de l'Eucharistie. C'est ce Sacrement que saint Jean appelle dans *l'Apocalypse* une manne cachée; et je crois qu'Isaïe le voyoit en cet estat, lorsqu'il dit en esprit de prophetie: Veritablement: tu es un Dieu caché." Pascal to Mlle Roannez, October 1656. *Œuvres*, t. vi, p. 88. *Pensées et Opuscules*, p. 214.

206 p. 84. See the last pages of the *Vie de M. Pascal*.

207 p. 84. Cf. "On ne peut faire une bonne phisionomie qu'en accordant toutes nos contrarietés, et il ne suffit pas de suivre une suite de qualités accordantes sans accorder les contraires." *Pensées*, no. 684.

"S'il y a jamais un temps auquel on doive faire profession des deux contraires c'est quand on reproche qu'on en omet un." *Pensées*, no. 865.

208 p. 85. Cf. "Ainsy il y a des proprietez communes à toutes choses, dont la connoissance ouvre l'esprit aux plus grandes merveilles de la nature. La principale comprend les deux infinitez qui se rencontrent dans toutes: l'une de grandeur, l'autre de petitesse.... En un mot... quelque mouvement, quelque nombre, quelque espace, quelque temps que ce soit, il y en a tousjours un plus grand et un moindre: de sorte qu'ils se soutiennent tous entre le neant et l'infiny, estant tousjours infiniment esloignez de ces extremes." *De l'esprit géométrique*, *Œuvres*, t. ix, pp. 255ff.; *Pensées et Opuscules*, p. 174.

"Le mouvement infini, le point qui remplit tout, le moment du repos: infini sans quantité, indivisible et infini." *Pensées*, no. 232.

209 p. 85. "La nature a mis toutes ses verités chacune en soy mesme; notre art les renferme les unes dans les autres, mais cela n'est pas naturel: chacune tient sa place." *Pensées*, no. 21.

210 p. 85. Cf. "Le pouvoir des roys sur les sujets n'est, ce me semble, qu'une image du pouvoir des esprits sur les esprits qui leur sont inferieurs, sur lesquels ils exercent le droit de persuader, qui est parmi eux ce que le droit de commander est dans le gouvernement politique. Ce second empire me paroist mesme d'un ordre d'autant plus elevé, que les esprits sont d'un ordre plus elevé que les corps, et d'autant plus equitable, qu'il ne peut estre desparti et conservé que par le merite, au lieu que l'autre peut l'estre par la naissance ou par la fortune." *Œuvres*, t. iii, p. 30; *Pensées et Opuscules*, p. 112.

211 p. 85. See above, pp. 18, 85, 111.

212 p. 86. Cf. "La grandeur de la sagesse, qui n'est nulle sinon de Dieu, est invisible aux charnels et aux gens d'esprit. Ce sont trois ordres differents de genre.

Les grands genies ont leur empire, leur esclat, leur grandeur, leur victoire, leur lustre, et n'ont nul besoing des grandeurs charnelles, où ils n'ont pas de raport. Ils sont veus non des yeux, mais des esprits, c'est assez.

Les saints ont leur empire, leur esclat, leur victoire, leur lustre, et n'ont nul besoin des grandeurs charnelles ou spirituelles, où elles n'ont nul rapport, car elles n'y ajoustent ny ostent. Ils sont veus de Dieu & des anges, et non des corps ny des esprits curieux. Dieu leur suffit.

Archimede sans esclat seroit en mesme veneration. Il n'a donné des batailles pour les yeux, mais il a fourny à tous les esprits ses inventions. O, qu'il a esclatté aux esprits.

J. C. sans biens & sans aucune production au dehors de science, est dans son ordre de sainteté. Il n'a point donné d'invention, il n'a point regné, mais il a esté humble, patient, saint, saint à Dieu, terrible aux demons, sans aucun pesché. O, qu'il est venu en grande pompe & en une prodigieuse magnificence aux yeux du cœur qui voyent la sagesse.

Il eust esté inutile à Archimede de faire le prince dans ses livres de geometrie quoyqu'il le fust.

Il eust esté inutile à N. S. J. C. pour esclatter dans son regne de sainteté, de venir en Roy, mais il y est bien venu avec l'esclat de son ordre.

Il est bien ridicule de se scandaliser de la bassesse de J. C. comme si cette bassesse est du mesme ordre, duquel est la grandeur qu'il venoit faire paroistre.......

Tous les corps, le firmament, les etoiles, la terre et ses royaumes, ne valent pas le moindre des esprits. Car il connoist tout cela, et soy, et les corps rien.

Tous les corps ensemble et tous les esprits ensemble et toutes leurs productions, ne vallent pas le moindre mouvement de charité. Cela est d'un ordre infiniment plus elevé.

De tous les corps ensemble, on ne sauroit en faire reussir une petite pensée, cela est impossible & d'un autre ordre. De tous les corps & esprits, on n'en scauroit tirer un mouvement de vraye charité, cela est impossible et d'un autre ordre surnaturel." *Pensées*, no. 793.

213 p. 87. "C'est le cœur qui sent Dieu, et non la raison. Voilà ce que c'est que la foy, Dieu sensible au cœur, non à la raison." *Pensées*, no. 278.

"Console-toi, tu ne me chercherois pas, si tu ne m'avois trouvé." *Pensées*, no. 553, "Le Mystère de Jesus."

214 p. 87. Cf. "Cœur, instinct, principes." *Pensées*, no. 281. "Le malheur est que ces principes appartiennent plus au cœur qu'à l'esprit, et que les hommes sont si peu accoutumés à étudier leur cœur, qu'il n'y a rien qui leur soit plus inconnu. Ce n'est presque jamais là que se portent leurs méditations; et quoiqu'ils ne fassent toute leur vie, et en toutes choses, que suivre les mouvemens de leur cœur, ce n'est que comme les aveugles," etc. *Discours sur les Pensées.*

"Non seulement les choses qu'il faut sentir dépendent du cœur, mais encore celles qui appartiennent à l'esprit, lorsque le cœur peut y avoir quelque part." *Discours sur les Pensées.*

"S'il n'y avoit rien d'incompréhensible que dans la Religion peut-être y auroit-il quelque chose à dire. Mais ce qu'il y a de plus connu dans la nature, c'est que presque tout ce que nous savons qui est, nous est inconnu, passé de certaines bornes, etc." *Ib.*

"Nous connoissons la verité, non seullement par la raison, mais encore par le cœur....Le cœur sent qu'il y a trois dimensions dans l'espace, et que les nombres sont infinis....Les principes se sentent, les propositions se concluent et le tout avec certitude quoique par differentes voies....Ceux à qui Dieu a donné la religion par sentiment de cœur sont bien heureux et bien legitimement persuadés." *Pensées*, no. 282.

215 p. 88. Cardinal Bérulle had introduced into France in 1604 her order of Reformed Carmelites. It is Pierre de l'Étoile who calls her *Life* "La Bible des Bigots." She was in great favour with the Port-Royalists, and Arnauld d'Andilly translated (but not till 1670) the first three volumes of her works. Cf. Lancelot, *op. cit.* t. i, p. 17.

216 p. 88. Cf. "Non enim per syllogismum sed per illuminationem interiorem aspiciunt veritatem, sicut interiores tenebrae et impuritas absque syllogismo inclinant hominem in falsitatem...qua propter novam condere Metaphysicam statuimus post ubi a deo errantes per flagella reducti sumus ad viam salutis et cognitionem divinorum, non per syllogismum, qui est quasi sagitta, qua scopum attingimus a longe absque gustu, sed neque modo per auctoritatem, quod est tangere quasi per manum alienam, sed per tactum intrinsecum in magna suavitate quam abscondit Deus timentibus se: modo certi de metaphysicis rebus facti audemus hominibus vias ostendere duce deo, de quo in theologicis tanquam salvatore et revelante ea quae nesciebamus alia ratione considerabimus." *Metaphysica* (Paris 1638), Procemium, pp. 4, 5.

By *tactus intrinsecus* Campanella means something more than conscience. It belongs to his theory of cognition, and is the foundation of his ontology and ethics. Its ethical content is due to the Thomistic doctrine of the moral origin of intellectual error.

On Campanella (1560–1639) see L. Amabile, *Fra Tommaso Campanella* (3 vols., Naples 1882), and B. Spaventa, *La filosofia italiana nelle sue relazione con la filosofia europea* (1909), pp. 86–95. Cf. also J. Kvačala, *Thomas Campanella. Ein Reformer der ausgehender Renaissance* (1909).

After long persecution he had fled to France, where he found a protector in Richelieu. His works were approved by the Sorbonne, and he was pensioned by Louis XIII. He knew Gassendi and Descartes, though the latter had no high opinion of him. His chief works published in France were

Astrologica (1629), *Medicinalia* (1635), *De praedestinatione ...Cento Thomisticus* (1636), *Atheismus Triumphatus* (1636), *Philosophia rationalis* (1638), *Philosophia universalis seu Metaphysica* (1638).

217 p. 88. Here are some passages which seem to indicate points of contact between Pascal and Cusanus.

(1) PASCAL: "Les sciences ont deux extremités qui se touchent, la premiere est la pure ignorance naturelle où se trouvent tous les hommes en naissant. L'autre extremité est celle où arrivent les grandes ames qui, ayants parcouru tout ce que les hommes peuvent sçavoir, trouvent qu'ils ne sçavent rien et se rencontrent en cette mesme ignorance d'où ils estoyent partis. Mais c'est une ignorance savante qui se connoist." *Pensées*, no. 327.

CUSANUS: "Profecto cum appetitus in nobis frustra non sit, desideramus scire nos ignorare. Hoc si ad plenum assequi poterimus, doctam ignorantiam assequemur. Nihil enim homini etiam studiosissimo, in doctrina perfectius adveniet quam in ipsa ignorantia quae ipsi propria est, doctissimum reperiri et tanto quis doctior est, quanto se magis sciverit ignorantem." *De docta ignorantia*, lib. I, cap. i.

(2) PASCAL: "(La conversion) consiste à connoistre qu'il y a une opposition invincible entre Dieu et nous; et que sans un mediateur il ne peut y avoir de commerce." *Pensées*, no. 470.

CUSANUS: "Quis non altissime rapitur, haec attentius prospiciens? Aperis enim tu, Deus meus, mihi misere tale occultum ut intuear hominem non posse te patrem intelligere, nisi in filio tuo qui est intelligibilis et mediator, etc." *De visione Dei*, cap. xix.

(3) PASCAL: "Car si nous ne passons par le milieu, nous ne trouverons en nous que de veritables malheurs, etc." Lettre à Mme Perier, 17 Oct. 1651, *Pensées et Opuscules*, p. 96.

CUSANUS: "Unde quamvis non possit fieri medium, cum sine medio non possit tibi uniri, etc." *De visione Dei*, cap. xix.

(4) PASCAL: "Le finy s'aneantyt en présence de l'infiny et devient un pur neant." *Pensées*, no. 233.

CUSANUS: "(Humana natura non potest transire in unionem cum divina essentialem) sicut finitum non potest infinito infinite uniri, transiret enim in identitatem infiniti et sic desiniret esse finitum quando de eo verificaretur infinitum." *De visione Dei*, cap. xx. "Finiti ad infinitum nulla est proportio." *Ib.* cap. xxiii.

(5) PASCAL: "*Deus absconditus*." *Pensées*, no. 194, no. 242, etc.

CUSANUS: "Videndo me, das te a me videri qui es Deus absconditus." *De visione Dei*, cap. v. "Deum esse absconditum, ab oculis omnium sapientum, scribitur, et omne invisibile in invisibili occultatur." *De ludi globo*, lib. II.

(6) PASCAL: "Tu ne me chercherois pas, si tu ne m'avois trouvé." *Pensées*, no. 553.

CUSANUS: "Nemo enim te videt, nisi qui te habet." *De visione Dei*, cap. vii. But cf. St Bernard: "Nemo te quaerere valet nisi qui prius invenerit." *De dilig. Deo*, vii. 22.

It is twenty years since M. E. Jovy signalized in the

Bulletin philologique et historique du Ministère de l'Instruction publique for 1895, the first two and most striking of these parallels. The subject has apparently not been pursued since, and has not received the attention which it deserves. It is too often assumed that Pascal was a man of three books, the Bible, Augustine, and Montaigne. The truth would seem that, without being a professed *érudit*, he was well abreast with the learning of his day.

Nicolaus of Coes or Cusa (Cusanus) (1401–1464), Cardinal, besides his political and ecclesiastical significance (see Creighton, *History of the Papacy*, vol. ii), merits particular attention as an anti-scholastic and mystic. He maintained that all human knowledge is conjecture (*De docta ignorantia*, 1440). We finite beings are incapable of comprehending the infinite or the truth and reality of things in their purity, for the True is never more or less, whereas our knowledge is capable of indefinite variety. So truth is constantly sought after, but never completely grasped, and all our knowledge is tinged with ignorance, and the deeper we plunge in ignorance, the nearer we attain to knowledge. Thus he taught the apprehension of God by "intentio speculativa." He was accused of Pantheism (*deus est omnia ut non possit esse aliud quam est*). Giordano Bruno, who developed his doctrines, called him "divine." He was a sound mathematician and physical philosopher, and anticipated Copernicus in the theory of the rotation of the earth. His works were edited by Jean Lefèvre d'Étaples in 1514.

See R. Falckenburg, *Grundzüge der Philosophie des Nic. Cusanus* (1880); F. J. Clemens, *Giordano Bruno und Nicolaus von Cusa* (1847), p. 45; F. A. Scharff, *Des Cardinals Nic. von Cusa wichtigste Schriften in deutscher Uebersetzung* (1862); J. M. Düx, *Der deutsche Card. Nic. von Cusa und die Kirche* (1847); V. Cantor, *Vorlesungen über die Geschichte der Mathematik* (1892), Bd ii, pp. 170 ff.

218 p. 88. Cf. "Pervenit (mens) ad id quod est in ictu trepidantis aspectus." *Conf.* VII, 17.

"Ex quo intelligitur quam nulla res in via tenere nos debeat, quando nec ipse dominus, in quantum via nostra esse dignatus est, tenere nos voluerit, sed transire, ne rebus temporalibus, quamvis ab illo pro salute nostra susceptis et gestis, haereamus infirmiter, sed per eas potius curramus alacriter, ut ad eum ipsum, qui nostram naturam a temporalibus liberavit et collocavit ad dexteram patris, provehi et pervehi mereamur."

De doctr. Christ. I, c. 34. See Harnack, *Dogmengeschichte* (E. tr.), vol. v, p. 99 *n.*

219 p. 89. The whole passage on the "Immanental Method" is founded on L. Laberthonnière's "L'apologétique et la méthode de Pascal" in his *Essais de Philosophie religieuse* (1903), pp. 193 ff. Cf. the same author's "Réponse à Monseigneur Turinaz" in *Annales de Philosophie Chrétienne*, tome i, pp. 398 ff.

220 p. 90. Cf. Mr James Thompson in *Hibbert Journal* for July 1914.

221 p. 90. "Ainsi sans l'escriture qui n'a que Jesus-Christ pour object, nous ne connoissons rien, et ne voyons qu'obscurité et confusion dans la nature de Dieu et dans la propre nature." *Pensées*, no. 548.

222 p. 91. "La Raison a beau crier; elle ne peut mettre le prix aux choses." *Pensées*, no. 82.

"La Raison nous commande bien plus imperieusement qu'un maistre; car en désobéissant à l'un on est malheureux, et en désobéissant à l'autre on est un sot." *Pensées*, no. 345.

"Travaillons donc à bien penser: voilà le principe de la morale." *Pensées*, no. 347.

223 p. 91. Cf. Wendland, J., *Miracles and Christianity* (1911), ch. i.

224 p. 91. Cf. Fr. von Hügel, *The Mystical Element in Religion* (1908), vol. i, p. 38.

225 p. 92. "L'homme n'agit point par la raison, qui fait son estre." *Pensées*, no. 439.

"L'homme par la grace est rendu semblable à Dieu et participant de sa divinité,...sans la grace il est comme semblable aux bestes brutes." *Pensées*, no. 434.

226 p. 92. 2 Cor. ii. 14; ix. 15.

227 p. 92. See above, note 122.

228 p. 93. "L'extreme vivacité de son esprit le rendoit si impatient quelques fois qu'on avoit peine à le satisfaire; mais dés aussy tost qu'on l'avertissoit, ou qu'il s'apercevoit luy mesme qu'il avoit fasché quelqu'un par cette impatience de son esprit, il reparoit incontinent sa faute par des traitements si honnestes qu'il n'a jamais perdu l'amitié de personne par là." *Vie de M. Pascal.*

229 p. 94. "'Ne me plaignez point; la maladie est l'estat naturel des Chrestiens parce qu'on est par là comme on devroit tousjours estre, c'est à dire dans la souffrance, dans les maux, dans la privation de tous les biens, et des plaisirs des sens, exempt de toutes les passions, sans ambition, sans avarice, et dans l'attente continuelle de la mort. N'est ce pas ainsi que les Chrestiens doivent passer leur vie? Et n'est ce pas un grand bonheur quand on est par nécessité dans un estat où l'on est obligé d'estre?... C'est pourquoy il ne nous demandoit autre chose que de prier Dieu qu'il lui fist cette grâce." *Vie de M. Pascal; Œuvres*, t. i, p. 109.

230 p. 94. Père Beurrier.

231 p. 94. "Mais la maxime qu'il s'estoit proposée de renoncer à toute sorte de superfluïtez estoit en luy un grand fondement de l'amour qu'il avoit pour la pauvreté. Une des choses sur quoi il s'examinoit le plus dans la veüe de cette maxime estoit sur cet excez general de vouloir exceller en tout, et qui nous portoit en particulier dans l'usage des choses du monde, à en vouloir tousjours avoir des meilleures, des plus belles, et des plus commodes. C'est pourquoy il ne pouvoit souffrir qu'on voulut se servir des meilleurs ouvriers; mais il nous disoit qu'il falloit tousjours chercher les plus pauvres et les plus gens de bien, et renoncer a cette excellence qui n'est jamais necessaire, et blasmoit fort aussi qu'on cherchast avec tant de soin d'avoir toutes ses commoditez comme d'avoir toutes choses prez de soy, une chambre où rien ne manquast, et autres choses de cette sorte que l'on fait sans scrupules; parce que, se reglant sur le fondement de l'esprit de pauvreté qui doit estre dans tous les chrestiens, il croioit que tout ce qui estoit opposé, quand mesme il seroit authorisé par l'usage de la bienseance du monde, estoit tousjours un excez à cause que nous y avons renoncé dans le baptesme. Il s'escrioit quelques fois 'Si j'avois le cœur aussi pauvre que l'esprit, je suis bien heureux; car je suis merveilleusement persuadé de l'esprit de pauvreté et que la pratique de cette vertu est un grand moyen pour faire son salut.'" *Vie de M. Pascal; Œuvres*, t. i, p. 87.

Cf. "C'est donc assurément un grand mal que d'estre dans le doute... celui qui doute et qui ne cherche pas est tout ensemble et bien malheureux et bien injuste; que s'il est avec cela tranquille et satisfait, qu'il en fasse profession, et enfin qu'il en fasse vanité, et que ce soit de cet estat mesme qu'il fasse le sujet de sa joye et de sa vanité, je n'ay point de termes pour qualifier une si extravagante créature." *Pensées*, no. 194.

232 p. 94. "Commencer par plaindre les incrédules: ils sont assez malheureux par leur condition. Il ne les faudroit injurier." *Pensées*, no. 189.

"Plaindre les athées qui cherchent, car ne sont ils pas assez malheureux! Invectiver contre ceux qui en font vanité." *Pensées*, no. 190.

"Je ne puis avoir que de la compassion pour ceux qui gemissent dans le doute," etc. *Pensées*, no. 194.

233 p. 96. "The subject of (the) Sermons shall be to shew the Evidence for Revealed Religion, and to demonstrate in the most convincing and persuasive manner the Truth and Excellence of Christianity." Extract from Mr John Hulse's Will.

INDEX

For EU product safety concerns, contact us at Calle de José Abascal, 56–1°, 28003 Madrid, Spain or eugpsr@cambridge.org.

www.ingramcontent.com/pod-product-compliance
Ingram Content Group UK Ltd.
Pitfield, Milton Keynes, MK11 3LW, UK
UKHW012332130625
459647UK00009B/238

* 9 7 8 1 1 0 7 6 2 8 9 4 6 *